MOUNTAIN BIKE *Here*

Ontario and Central & Western New York

SUE LEBRECHT

The BOSTON
MILLS PRESS

Cataloguing in Publication Data

Lebrecht, Sue, 1962-
    Mountain bike here: Ontario and Central & Western New York

ISBN 1-55046-292-X

1. All terrain cycling – Ontario - Guidebooks.
2. All terrain cycling – New York (State) – Guidebooks.
3. Trails – Ontario – Guidebooks.
4. Trails – New York (State) – Guidebooks.
5. Ontario – Guidebooks.
6. New York (State) – Guidebooks.
I. Title.

GV1046.C32057 1999b   796.6'3'09713   99-930274-4

Copyright © 1999 Sue Lebrecht

03 02 01 00 99   1 2 3 4 5

Published in 1999 by
Boston Mills Press
132 Main Street
Erin, Ontario N0B 1T0
Tel 519-833-2407
Fax 519-833-2195
e-mail books@boston-mills.on.ca
www.boston-mills.on.ca

An affiliate of
Stoddart Publishing Co. Limited
34 Lesmill Road
Toronto, Ontario, Canada
M3B 2T6
Tel 416-445-3333
Fax 416-445-5967
e-mail gdsinc@genpub.com

Distributed in Canada by
General Distribution Services Limited
325 Humber College Boulevard
Toronto, Canada M9W 7C3
Orders 1-800-387-0141 Ontario & Quebec
Orders 1-800-387-0172 NW Ontario & Other Provinces
e-mail customer.service@ccmailgw.genpub.com
EDI Canadian Telebook S1150391

Distributed in the United States by
General Distribution Services Inc.
85 River Rock Drive, Suite 202
Buffalo, New York 14207-2170
Toll-free 1-800-805-1083
Toll-free fax 1-800-481-6207
e-mail gdsinc@genpub.com
www.genpub.com
PUBNET 6307949

All photographs by the author.

Design by Joseph Gisini, Andrew Smith Graphics Inc.
Printed in Canada

*Boston Mills Press gratefully acknowledges the Canada Council for the Arts, the Government
of Canada through the Book Publishing Industry Development Program (BPIDP), and the
Ontario Arts Council for their support of our publishing program.*

A portion of sales proceeds from this book will go to trail maintenance and advocacy.

●

Dedicated to all the mountain bikers who showed this stranger their favorite legal riding haunts in return for beer and ice cream.

Contents

Acknowledgments 9

Introduction... 11
   Fat-tire Revolution 12
   Rules of the Trail.. 13
   Getting Along 14
   Ratings 15

ONTARIO • Central
1 Dagmar Mountain Bike Centre 18
2 Durham Forest 20
3 Ravenshoe.. 23
4 Scanlon Creek Conservation Area 26
5 Coulson's Hill 28
6 Caledon Trailway... 30
7 Kelso Conservation Area... 33
8 Hilton Falls Conservation Area 36
9 Elora Cataract Trailway.. 38
10 Ganaraska Forest Centre Ski Trails............................... 41
11 Victoria Rail Trail... 43
12 Hardwood Hills Mountain Bike Centre 46
13 North Simcoe Rail Trail.. 48
14 Mansfield Outdoor Centre 51
15 Kolapore Uplands 54

ONTARIO • West
16 Ted's Range Road Diner 58
17 Inglis Falls Conservation Area..................................... 61
18 MacGregor Point Provincial Park 64
19 Guelph Lake 66
20 Dundas Valley Conservation Area 69
21 Hamilton-to-Brantford Rail Trail 72
22 Cambridge-to-Paris Rail Trail 75
23 The Pines... 78
24 Boler Mountain 81
25 Short Hills Provincial Park... 83

ONTARIO • East

26 Northumberland Forest 88

27 Goodrich-Loomis Conservation Area...............................91

28 Macaulay Mountain Conservation Area...........................93

29 Silent Lake Provincial Park 96

30 Kanata Lakes..99

31 Camp Fortune 102

32 Gatineau Park...104

ONTARIO • North Central

33 Porcupine Ridge...108

34 Bracebridge Resource Management Centre.......................111

35 Moose Woods Trail Centre...114

36 Haliburton Forest...116

37 Rocky Crest Resort...118

38 Grandview Inn Nature Trails..121

39 Algonquin's Minnesing Mountain Bike Trail 124

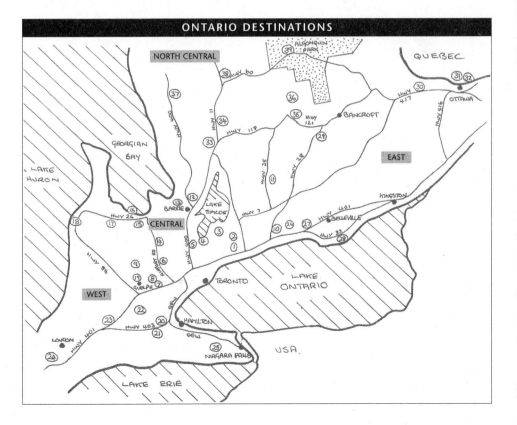

ONTARIO DESTINATIONS

NEW YORK • West

40 Holiday Valley, Holimont, and Rock City 130
41 Alleghany State Park...133
42 Sprague Brook Park...135
43 Erie County Forest...137
44 Letchworth State Park..140
45 Rattlesnake Hill...143
46 Spencer Park...146

NEW YORK • Central

47 Bear Swamp...152
48 Highland Forest..154
49 Stoney Pond..157
50 Vanderkamp Center..160
51 Barnes Corners...163

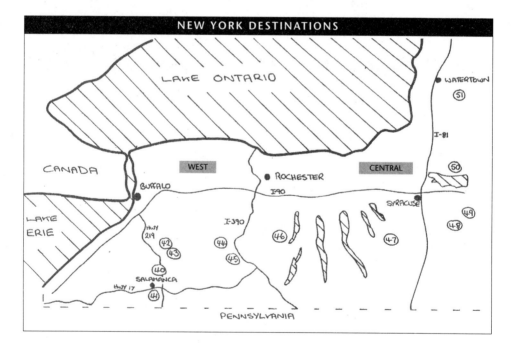

Appendices

Ontario Cycling Association..166
New York Mountain Biking Coalition 167

Acknowledgments

Writing is my mission, my official business that allows me to play as much as I do on my mountain bike.

Playing is infinitely more fun with friends. I'd like to thank Lisa Dost and Dave Hiscox, Steve Jarrett, John Moulton, and Jeff Waller for joining me on various biking expeditions. They crammed into stuffed cars, rode back up hills so I could photograph them, waited patiently while I stopped to jot notes, and added fun and laughter.

Word of mouth, the internet, and the Ontario Cycling Association steered me to mountain bike-active shops, clubs and associations, and too many people to mention. They in turn led me to "their" trails. I never biked alone. Thank you for your time, your insights to trails and trail issues, for your hand-drawn maps, and for providing me with one heck of an incredible bike season.

Of special mention is Jon Sundquist, my first and foremost contact in New York State. He is a strong advocacy voice in the mountain bike community. He is trails chair for the Western New York Mountain Bike Association, the chairman for the New York Mountain Bike Coalition, and the New York State representative for the International Mountain Biking Association. Jon Sundquist not only showed me some great riding spots, but also pointed me in all the right directions — to people and places — in a vast area I knew nothing about. For providing me with short cuts, accurate information and political sensitivities surrounding mountain biking in your state — thank you.

For financial assistance, I'd like to thank Ontario Tourism. And for accommodations in New York, I'd like to thank Greater Rochester Visitors Association and the Syracuse Convention and Visitors Bureau.

Introduction

Mountain Bike Here is a mountain biking trail guide to 51 legal off-road riding hot spots, 39 of them in Southern Ontario and 12 in Central and Western New York State.

Mountain Bike Here features maps, site descriptions, directions, ratings, tips, cautions, restrictions, group ride and club contacts, clinics and tours, regional tourism numbers, and a host of other quickly accessible, user-friendly information.

Moreover, it is a fully sanctioned guide, accredited by the Ontario Cycling Association and the New York Mountain Biking Coalition. A portion of proceeds from sales of this book goes toward trail advocacy and maintenance through these two groups.

Trails presented here are favorites. Diverse in their virtues, they are the choice sites of active riders. I researched this book through bike shops, clubs and associations, and a heck of a lot of pedaling.

What is a "best" trail? Everyone has his or her own perspective of a great trail. Some riders like to know fear and test their skills on highly technical terrain. Some revel in rhythm on smooth, swoopy singletrack. Others crave tough workouts with hills and distance. Appreciations vary, widely and significantly. Mountain biking is a thrill, a sport, a pastime, an exercise, a mode of exploration, a cool sensation, and whatever else that gets you motivated.

This book features trail parks designed by mountain bikers for mountain bikers. It offers destinations worth a drive where you can ride, camp, swim and enjoy other activities. You will find wilderness parks, competition sites and local hot spots. Rides vary from easy off-road initiation areas, to six rail-trail corridors loaded with history, and scenic routes that take in waterfalls, wildflowers, butterflies, birds and high points with vistas for fall colors. Presenting tight singletrack, wide singletrack, and doubletrack, this book is for kamikaze cyclists, cruisers, sweethearts and families. I've included secure, mapped, marked routes as well as complex, remote networks where compasses are required.

Legal welcoming bike trails can be found in provincial parks, conservation areas, public forest tracts, private land, cross-country and alpine ski resorts, rail trails, state forests, state recreation areas and wildlife management areas.

From one perspective, this book is a guide to several innovative and successful marriages of bikes to land.

Scores of ski resorts — both alpine and cross-country — have opened their properties to singletrack trail development; see Boler Mountain, Holiday Valley, Hardwood Hills, Dagmar Mountain Bike Centre, Mansfield Outdoor Centre and Camp Fortune.

Private land owners, approached by individuals and bike-shop owners, have allowed the creation of trail parks on their property; see Ted's Range Road Diner, Porcupine Ridge and Vanderkamp Center.

The Ministry of Natural Resources approved trail development by race organizers in specific forest tracts; see Ravenshoe, Durham Forest and Coulson's Hill. Macaulay Mountain Conservation Area allowed a bike club to reclaim of old trails on its property.

The Woodstock Cycling Club leases a piece of land on a conservation area for its trail park; see the Pines. The network at Guelph Lake is the creation of the Guelph Off-Road Bicycling Association, formed when the Grand River Conservation Authority granted multi-use trail development on a chunk of land.

I've personally biked on each site. Through the mud, sweat, and gears of countless miles (and kilometers), I've tried to help you plan your ideal off-road riding trips. Everything here is correct at the time of publication. Trails, however, change all the time. Bad weather knocks down trees, and politics places restrictions. It's always best to call for updates.

Fat-Tire Revolution

Mountain biking has come a long way in a short time with a big impact. When we first got our fat tires and set tracks off-road in the woods we reveled in the boundless possibilities and hit trails everywhere. The sport caught on and we multiplied. But then problems surfaced.

In wet conditions, we wore deep grooves in the earth. When we skirted puddles we widened trails. When we zipped by hikers, we intruded on their solitude. And one by one, trails closed to bike use.

So we turned our wheels to the issues and got organized. Trail advocacy groups formed, in Canada, in Ontario, and in New York State, including the International Mountain Biking Association (IMBA), the Ontario Recreational Mountain Bicycle Alliance (ORMBA), the Canadian Mountain Bicycling Alliance (CMBA), the Western New York Mountain Biking Association (WNYMBA), and the New York Mountain Biking Coalition (NYMBC).

These groups, among many others, all strive to prevent trail closures, minimize fat-tire impact on trails, and promote trail repair and maintenance. They set up booths at bicycling shows, hand out pamphlets on etiquette, organize bike patrols, maintenance and clean-up days, and communicate with land managers and hiking groups.

Indeed, a lot of trails are open through sheer good public relations. People with a passion for biking — volunteers mostly — strike up a respectful rapport with land managers and convince them that mountain bikers are a responsible group.

Which we are.

Rules of the Trail

Thousands of miles of dirt trails are closed to mountain bicyclists. The irresponsible riding habits of a few riders have contributed to this. Do your part to maintain trail access by observing the following rules of the trail, formulated by IMBA, the International Mountain Bicycling Association. IMBA's mission is to promote environmentally sound and socially responsible mountain bicycling.

RIDE ON OPEN TRAILS ONLY

Respect trail and road closures. Ask if not sure. Avoid possible trespass on private land, obtain permits or other authorization as may be required. Federal, most provincial, and state wilderness areas are closed to cycling. The way you ride will influence trail management decisions and policies.

LEAVE NO TRACE

Be sensitive to the dirt beneath you. Even on open, or legal, trails, do not ride under certain conditions. Recognize different types of soils, what happens after rain, and trail construction; practice low-impact cycling. Stay on existing trails and do not create new ones. Don't cut switchbacks. Pack out at least as much as you pack in.

CONTROL YOUR BICYCLE

Inattention for even a second can cause accidents. Obey all bicycle speed regulations and recommendations.

ALWAYS YIELD TRAIL

Make known your approach well in advance. A friendly greeting or bell is considerate and works well; don't startle others. Show your respect when passing; slow to a walking pace or even stop. Anticipate other trail users around corners or in blind spots.

NEVER SPOOK ANIMALS

All animals are startled by an unannounced approach, a sudden movement, or a loud noise. This can be dangerous for you, others, and the animals. Give animals extra room and time to adjust to you. When passing horses use special care and follow directions from the horseback riders. Ask if uncertain. Running cattle and disturbing wildlife is a serious offense. Leave gates as you found them, or as marked.

PLAN AHEAD

Know your equipment, your ability, and the area in which you are riding — and prepare accordingly. Be self-sufficient at all times. Keep your equipment in good repair and carry necessary supplies for changes in weather or other conditions. A well-prepared trip is a satisfaction to you and not a burden or offense to others. Always wear a helmet and appropriate safety gear.

Keep trails open by setting a good example of environmentally sound and socially responsible off-road cycling.

IMBA, PO Box 7578, Boulder, CO 80306-7578 USA
303-545-9011, fax 303-545-9026, e-mail imba@aol.com, www.imba.com

Getting Along

You are an ambassador of our sport.

HIKER ETIQUETTE

Say hi to hikers, smile, and if they yield to your approach, thank them and pass slowly — very slowly. You don't want them going home with stories of "I almost got run over by a bike" or "I had to jump out of their way."

HORSE ETIQUETTE

Horses are easily spooked. When approaching a horse, call out to the rider and ask, "Is your horse okay with bicycles?" Pull off the trail and let the horse go by. Be sure to speak, so the horse identifies you as human. Do not remove your helmet as this has been known to spook horses.

BIKE ETIQUETTE

Bikers are not impressed if you speed past them — even when you feel you are in complete control. Slow down.

USE YOUR FRONT BRAKE

Your front brake has far more stopping power than the rear. It won't lock up and slide, causing damage to the trail. Do not use your rear brake to skid-turn.

MAINTAIN TRAILS

If a tree branch or other debris — clearly not part of the trail design — presents an obstacle, take a moment and clear it from the trail. Volunteer for trail maintenance and clean-up days. Invest some sweat equity.

RESPECT THE HONOR SYSTEM

A lot of trail sites closed to bikes are not posted with "No Biking" signs, nor are they patrolled by law enforcement. Only bike where you know you're allowed.

REPORT ABUSE

If you see someone causing damage to the forest — dumping refuse, cutting trees, operating motor vehicles where prohibited — contact the land manager or police. Get a license plate number if you can.

JOIN THE CLUB

If you love to bike, don't take trail access for granted. Get involved with a bike club or association.

Ratings

Under the heading of each destination, the following symbols indicate the type of riding available. Many destinations offer a variety of trails with varying difficulties, noted by multi-symbols.

EASY
Gentle rolling, wide, non-technical doubletrack.
Minor rocky sections and/or sand patches.

INTERMEDIATE
Hills. Singletrack. Roots, rocks, logs, mud.

ADVANCED
Tough, demanding climbs, fast downhills, steep gnarly descents, challenging technical sections

EXPERT
Superior bike-handling skills required. Strong tolerance for pain an asset. Sense of humor necessary.

In the Ratings section of each destination, "Technical" refers to the intensity of roots, rocks, logs, steeps and other nasties. It does not take hills, elevation and length into account.

Directions are generally provided from major highways, but your approach may be different, depending on your location. Locate the site on a map before heading out.

Maps are overviews, providing a sense of play and the lay of the land. Most are not to scale and many do not include all spurs and offshoots. At some sites, detailed maps are available.

Note all Politics, Restrictions and Cautions before hitting the trail.

Ontario

Mansfield Outdoor Centre

Dagmar Mountain Bike Centre ①

■ ◆ ◆◆ NORTH OF AJAX

Ratings

LENGTH: 20 km (12.5 miles)

TRAIL: Singletrack and doubletrack

SURFACE: Hardpacked earth

TECHNICAL: Moderate to extreme

LAYOUT: Well-marked and mapped, doubletrack loop with singletrack offshoots

TOPOGRAPHY: Forested hills and ravines of the Oak Ridges Moraine

AESTHETICS: High leafy canopy, mature trees, and wildflowers

IMPRESSION: Technical satisfaction with fun and flurry

Site of a Wednesday night race series and host to Ontario Cup and Enduro Cup races, Dagmar has established itself as a seriously fun playground. Set in the forested hills and ravines of the Oak Ridges Moraine, the Centre offers a great doubletrack rollercoaster with a variety of singletrack options.

The layout is simple. The doubletrack is a 10 km (6 mile) main loop. From it, singletrack offshoots form a variety of additional loops, parallel alternatives, and bypasses. None of the offshoots are long, yet all are technical.

The entire network is well signed, mapped, skill-rated, and one-way. The doubletrack, marked green, is hardpacked, delightfully smooth and cleared of broken branches. It's fast, but demanding with quad-buster climbs that pay back with thrilling downhills.

The singletrack offshoots are rated blue for difficult and red for expert. There are 15 possibilities — a total of 10 km (6 miles). Designed by Chico Racing, these trails twist and turn through roots, logs, washboard ground, and rocky ravines. Expert trails like Chico Wilde Ride, North Shore and Ogre's Home Brew, dare even the most adroit biker with drop-offs, severe climbs, and acute turns down steep descents.

Status

POLITICS: Dagmar Mountain Bike Centre is a cross-country and alpine center in winter.

ETIQUETTE: Helmets are mandatory.

EVENTS: Spring Ontario Cup; Enduro Cup 2; Dagmar Derailleur Destroyer; Wednesday Night Race Series, all presented by Chico Racing, 905-852-0381.

Guide Notes

NEAREST COMMUNITY: Uxbridge, Ajax, Stouffville

LOCATION: From Toronto, take Highway 401 east from Toronto to Harwood Avenue in Ajax. Go north to Highway 2, east 5 km (3 miles) to Lakeridge Road, then north 19 km (12 miles).

FACILITIES: Vending machines, washrooms, and bike wash. Cycling camps and camping for groups.

TRAIL MAP: Available on-site.

ADMISSION: Trail pass is $5 for adults, $3 children age 12 and under, season passes available. Open May to mid-October, weekends and holidays only, from 9 A.M. to 5 P.M.

REPAIR SHOP: Boyd's Source for Sports, 5402 Main Street, Suite 201, Stouffville, 905-640-6657. Northern Cycle, 889 Westney Road S., Ajax, 905-619-8875. Impala Cycles, 185 Thickson Road, Whitby, 905-434-4530.

TOURISM INFORMATION: Tourism Durham, 800-413-0017 or 905-723-0023.

LAND MANAGER: Dagmar Resort, 905-649-2002 or 905-649-2003.

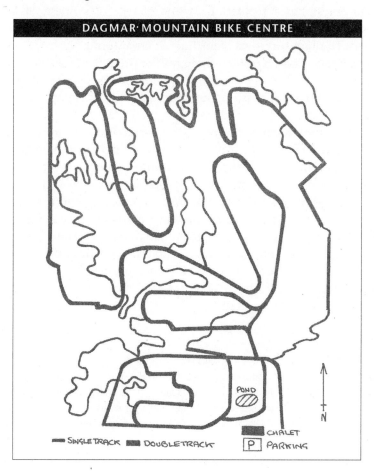

Durham Forest ②

Ratings

LENGTH: 25 km (15.5 miles)

TRAIL: Singletrack and doubletrack

SURFACE: Hardpack with a few sandy patches

TECHNICAL: Moderate to extreme

LAYOUT: Unmarked network

TOPOGRAPHY: Hilly mixed forest

AESTHETICS: Huge pines, leafy undergrowth, valleys, and possible deer encounters

IMPRESSION: Blueprint singletrack

Durham Forest has a reputation as one of Ontario's finest fat-tire playgrounds. Featuring singletrack trails designed by mountain bikers for mountain bikers, Durham Forest, its Main Tract, is enrapturing.

Set like a roller coaster in the rolling hills of the Oak Ridges Moraine, trails wind you up and let you loose. Well-worn paths lead you up slopes, along ridges and down valleys — swooping under a high leafy canopy and between thick trunks of pines.

The constant undulation of kinetic dips is matched with long ascents and proportionate downhills. With the exception of one technical section in the south end, affectionately referred to as Demon Forest with its rooty alley, the trail is a soft and smooth, hardpacked, extremely well drained, pine-needle-strewn playway. Catch a rhythm and you will keep it for hours.

Can you get lost? Yes. But three roads and a private fence along the south border frame the square-shaped property. A radio tower stands on the highest point of land near the southwest. When you want out, head to the tower, and take the gravel doubletrack west to the 7th Concession and turn right to return to the parking lot. The 370-ha (914 acre) property also offers an extensive network of doubletrack trails.

Status

POLITICS: The success of this mountain bike mecca is due largely to Chico Racing, organizers of the Superfly Ontario Cup, held annually at this site since 1993. To run the event, Chico Racing develops, maintains and cleans trails, under the watchful eye of the Ministry of Natural Resources. Management of the forest may revert back to the Municipality of Durham, so changes may occur. Hikers and equestrians frequent the forest.

ETIQUETTE: Don't bike in April when the ground is muddy.

EVENTS: Superfly Ontario Cup (also includes neighboring private trails), late spring, organized by Chico Racing, 905-852-0381. Enduro Cup 1, Uxbridge Icebreaker, early spring, organized by Bikenxs, 905-852-5544.

MAINTENANCE: A trail clean-up day is organized each spring by Chico Racing.

CAUTIONS: Unmarked, trails are two-way; make yourself known on blind corners and downhills. Poison ivy exists in some areas.

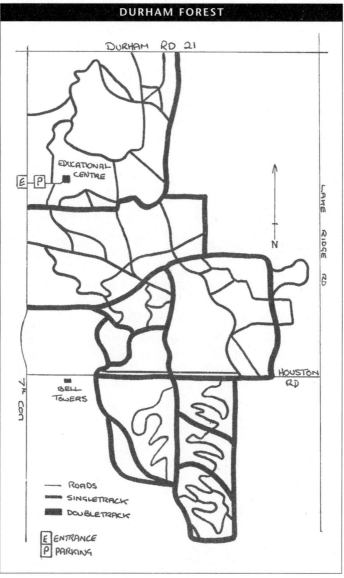

Trail map courtesy of Dave LaPointe

Guide Notes

NEAREST COMMUNITY: Uxbridge

LOCATION: From Highway 401 east of Toronto, go east to Brock Road (Regional Road 1) in Pickering, go north to Coppin's Corners, east on Durham Road 21 for 5 km (3 miles) to 7th Concession Road, turn right. Entrance is 1 km (0.6 miles) south on the left-hand side.

TRAIL MAP: On Internet at http://webhome.idirect.com/~lapointe

FACILITIES: Limited parking

ADMISSION: Free

TIPS: Get initiated with someone who knows the trails. Wear bug repellent.

REPAIR SHOP: Boyd's Source for Sports, 5402 Main Street, Suite 201, Stouffville, 905-640-6657. Northern Cycle, 889 Westney Road S., Ajax, 905-619-8875. Impala Cycles, 185 Thickson Road, Whitby, 905-434-4530.

TOURISM INFORMATION: Tourism Durham, 800-413-0017 or 905-723-0023.

LAND MANAGER: Ministry of Natural Resources, 905-713-7395.

Ravenshoe

Ravenshoe ③

■ ◆ ◆◆ SOUTHEAST OF KESWICK

Ratings

LENGTH: 15 km (9 miles)

TRAIL: Singletrack

SURFACE: Hardpack with roots, obstacles, and bridges

TECHNICAL: Moderate to extreme

LAYOUT: Unmarked network

TOPOGRAPHY: Rolling terrain with hardwood forest and pine plantation

AESTHETICS: Hills and dales with different forested pockets

IMPRESSION: Fat-tire funhouse requiring finesse

Ravenshoe is a technical playground with tight track, twisty turns, roots, logs, ramps and steeps. Intermediates are challenged to ride a clean game in this terrain.

Though a spring race is held here, Ravenshoe doesn't ride like a fast track. Trails are intimate and flavorful. Take your time, as you would in a fine restaurant, savoring the taste while looking pretty and keeping composed. Routes are stylish, rhythmic, and thoughtfully laid out for spicy satisfaction.

Officially, Ravenshoe is the Brown Hill Tract of York Regional Forest. A restless transplant from B.C.'s Okanagan Valley developed its trails. With forest management approval, Mister Restless — who prefers to remain anonymous — followed his yellow Labrador retriever down ravines, along ridges, among trees in loamy soil. As his lab sniffed out former deer and hunting trails, Restless raked and pruned.

He avoided fragile sandy areas, built sturdy innovative bridges over creeks, and placed rubber snowmobile tread over muddy spots and steep ascents for traction and to minimize erosion. The more he developed, the more technically challenging he schemed. There are endless fiery dips and kinetic rhythmic rolls.

The Raven's 10 km (6 miles) of trails snake through different forest pockets. The Pine Loop meanders through needle plantation. The Bellringer swoops among hardwoods. The Worm weaves a ravine with a set of switchbacks. Routes come close to each another, though you wouldn't know it to bike it. To the south, Old Jays is a twisty, off-chamber, bronco ride, while Stinky, set among cedars, is the most technical of all.

Set within a not-so-large, 89-ha (35 acre) property, trails roam between fireroads that form the shape of an H. This doubletrack offers a breather as you string the trails together.

Ravenshoe

Status

POLITICS: The Land Manager supports the trail maintenance by the organizers of the Ravenshoe Enduro. It has improved and expanded the access parking lot and has offered to pay for bridge material and the production of a trail map. Hikers and equestrians frequent the trails.

RESTRICTIONS: The big open field with a motorcross track adjacent to the forest in the south is private property; don't trespass.

ETIQUETTE: Make an effort to clear debris from the track.

EVENTS: Ravenshoe Enduro, held in spring, contact Spoke O' Motion, 905-853-9545.

MAINTENANCE: Call to volunteer for the spring clean-up day and receive a jacket patch from York Regional Forest.

CAUTIONS: Two-way traffic and blind corners.

Guide Notes

NEAREST COMMUNITY: Keswick

LOCATION: Take Highway 404 north from Toronto, take Exit 51 on Davis Drive (Regional Road 31). Go east 9 km (5.5 miles) to Highway 48, then north 14.5 km (9 miles) to Ravenshoe Road. Go west 2 km (1.2 miles) to McCowan Road, then south 0.6 km (0.4 miles) to the entrance on the right-hand side.

TRAIL MAP: Not available

FACILITIES: Limited parking

ADMISSION: Free for now, but the Land Manager suggests a $10 maintenance donation in a drop box at the parking lot.

REPAIR SHOP: Spoke O' Motion, 17915 Leslie Street N., Unit 2, Newmarket, 905-853-9545.

TOURISM INFORMATION: Georgina Leisure Services Dept., 905-476-4301.

LAND MANAGER: York Regional Forest of the Ministry of Natural Resources, 905-895-1231.

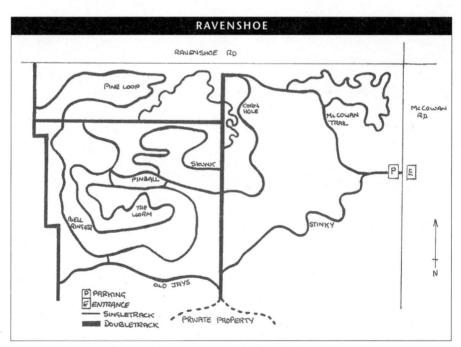

Trail map courtesy of Mister Restless

Scanlon Creek Conservation Area ④

Ratings

LENGTH: 10 km (6 miles)

TRAIL: Singletrack

SURFACE: Hardpack with muddy patches

TECHNICAL: Moderate

LAYOUT: Unmarked network

TOPOGRAPHY: Hilly, wooded land with meadows around a reservoir

AESTHETICS: Diverse terrain and in a small area, spring wildflowers, and high points with picturesque views of fall colors

IMPRESSION: Limited trails in a pretty little setting

A maze of singletrack trails laces this small, hilly, and pretty park. They run through high open fields and maple forest, down steep slopes into lowlands among cedars and hemlock.

A main loop runs beside Scanlon Creek and around the park's reservoir in the northeast end. Bridges cross the creek and boardwalks provide passage over muddy patches. Numerous offshoots from this circuit meet with a host of other trails that stem from the access road running three-quarters of the way around the park's perimeter.

Trails are unmarked, but you'll figure out the lay of the land within an hour. The trail map is out-of-date. While it provides an idea of the network, some trails have been re-routed while others are overgrown.

Status

POLITICS: Trails are heavily used by hikers.

ETIQUETTE: Take all descents slowly. Avoid biking on trails around the reservoir after a rainfall. Check trail conditions with park staff.

EVENTS: Site to an annual race, call Spoke O' Motion, 905-853-9545.

Guide Notes

NEAREST COMMUNITY: Bradford

LOCATION: Take Highway 400 north from Toronto to Highway 88 east to downtown Bradford, then Highway 11 north for 4 km (2.5 miles) to the 9th Concession, turn right and follow signs.

TRAIL MAP: Out-of-date, available from the Land Manager.

FACILITIES: Washrooms, drinking water, swimming, picnic tables, barbecues, camping for groups with reservations.

ADMISSION: $7.50 per vehicle

TIPS: Bring your swimsuit and take an after-ride plunge in the reservoir, which has a sandy beach. Wear bug repellent. Ride mid-week to avoid crowds.

REPAIR SHOP: Spoke O' Motion, 17915 Leslie Street N., Unit 2, Newmarket, 905-853-9545.

TOURISM INFORMATION: Bradford & District Chamber of Commerce, 905-775-3037.

LAND MANAGER: Lake Simcoe Region Conservation Authority, 905-895-1281.

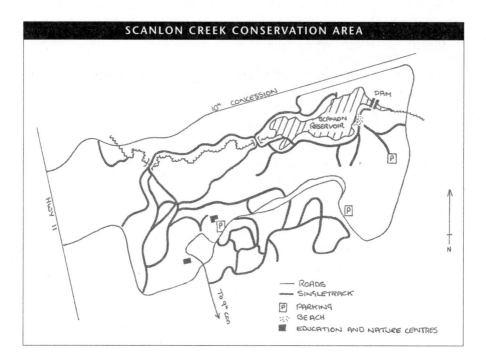

SCANLON CREEK CONSERVATION AREA

Coulson's Hill (5)

Ratings

LENGTH: 10 km (6 miles)

TRAIL: Singletrack

SURFACE: Hardpack

TECHNICAL: Moderate

LAYOUT: Well-signed loop (from mid-April to the end of August)

TOPOGRAPHY: Relatively flat pine forest

AESTHETICS: Dark woods

IMPRESSION: A short, sweet, fast, twisty blast

Thanks to a regularly held Tuesday night race series, red arrows lead the way through pine forest on a 5- to 8-km-long (3–5 mile) loop. The route twists and turns between pines and undulates over humps and mounds. Riders face little creek crossings, log obstacles and rock piles, but you can nevertheless catch a rhythm and ride fast.

The course changes every two weeks, so that keeps it interesting — while minimizing trail wear — and provides possibilities beyond the marked route. Moreover, when the race series finishes at the end of September, you'll be on your own — without red arrows pointing the way.

But go ahead, explore. All trails eventually cross the fireroad, which streaks through the center of the property from the 11th to the 12th Line. If you feel lost, follow the fireroad south back to the parking lot — listening for Highway 400 to the west.

Officially called the Hodgson Tract of Simcoe County Forest, riders refer to the forest as Coulson's Hill in reference to its access road, the 11th Line. Contrary to its name, the property doesn't have a hill — just a lot of roly-poly dips.

Status

POLITICS: The forest is open to all non-motorized recreation.

EVENTS: Tuesday night race series, mid-April to the end of August, organized by Spoke O' Motion, 905-853-9545.

CAUTIONS: Poison ivy in sections. Open to hunters during hunting season in spring and fall.

Guide Notes

NEAREST COMMUNITY: Bradford

LOCATION: Take Highway 400 north from Toronto to Highway 88 and go east 2.3 km (1.5 miles) to Sideroad 10. Then go north 5.5 km (3.5 miles) to the 11th Line, and west 2 km (1.2 miles). The parking lot is on the north side of the road just before the Highway 400 bridge. (Don't drive into the woods at the Simcoe Forest sign, but proceed past it to the lot.)

TRAIL MAP: Not available

FACILITIES: Limited parking

ADMISSION: Free

TIPS: Route arrows are removed in September.

REPAIR SHOP: Spoke O' Motion, 17915 Leslie Street N., Unit 2, Newmarket, 905-853-9545.

TOURISM INFORMATION: Bradford & District Chamber of Commerce, 905-775-3037.

LAND MANAGER: Simcoe County, Forest Department, 905-729-2294.

Mansfield Outdoor Centre

Caledon Trailway ⑥

Ratings

LENGTH: 36 km (22 miles)

TRAIL: Rail trail

SURFACE: Hardpack, sandy sections

TECHNICAL: Easy

LAYOUT: Straight corridor

TOPOGRAPHY: Credit River Valley, Oak Ridges Moraine

AESTHETICS: Wooden trestles, small towns, Niagara Escarpment views, wetland overlook

IMPRESSION: Exercise and ice cream

The Caledon Trailway stretches 36 km (22 miles) from Terra Cotta east to Palgrave. It links small towns and cuts through countryside, alternatively running past backyards and farms, then among forests, fields and wetland.

Doubletrack leads in and out of towns, but otherwise the trail is narrow, accommodating single-file riding in a 3-meter-wide (10 foot) swath of grass. With the exception of a 5-km (3 mile) stretch of loose sandy soil between Kennedy Road and St. Andrews Road, the trail is firm and hardpacked. A succession of undulations in the west adds fun.

Under the brow of the Niagara Escarpment, the western third runs through the Credit River Valley through large wetland complexes and open fields. Before Cheltenham, you'll pass the old Brick Works factory, a ghostly site of eerie-looking buildings. After Inglewood, you'll have a clear view of the Devil's Pulpit, a prominent rise of land on the Escarpment steeped in native lore.

The middle section edges an ancient lake bed, now the ground for fruit farms and hardwood forest. It includes a large stand of stately black walnut, easily recognized by their thick trunks, 9-meter (30 foot) branches and dangling walnuts in fall.

The Oak Ridges Moraine encompasses the final third, where hills upon hills can be seen on both sides of the trail. East of Palgrave, you'll ride on an elevated tract with radical drops on either side. Sandstone benches invite you to stop and spy on flocks of birds congregating in the spruce bog, 11 meters (36 feet) below.

A total of seven historic wooden trestles provide passage over backroads and running water — including the Credit and Little Credit Rivers and Centreville Creek. Large signs at major road crossings display trail maps and list en route sites. But the sweetest reward is ice cream and baked goodies at towns along with way. Two choice spots are Terra Cotta and Inglewood.

The Caledon Trailway used to be a rail line that linked Hamilton with Barrie from the 1870s to 1967. Today, this multi-use recreational corridor is part of the Trans Canada Trail with a link to the Elora Cataract Trailway in the works.

At Caledon East, a pavilion acknowledges the names of thousands who have made donations toward the coast-to-coast project. A park with native tree plantings and wetland re-creations surround it.

Status

POLITICS: Owned by the Town of Caledon, this multi-use recreational trail is frequented by hikers and equestrians.

EVENTS: Caledon Trailway Day, the Saturday closest to June 21.

MAINTENANCE: Town of Caledon Parks Department with Caledon Trailway volunteers.

CAUTIONS: Use extreme caution at the road crossings of Highway 10, Airport Road, and Old Church Road.

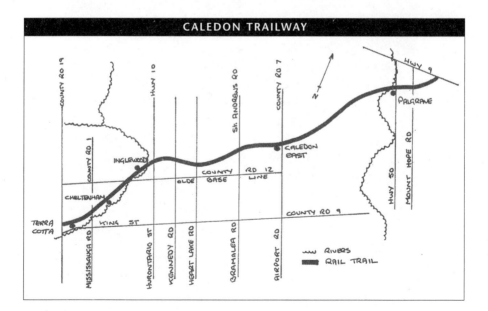

Guide Notes

NEAREST COMMUNITY: Terra Cotta, Cheltenham, Inglewood, Caledon East, Palgrave

LOCATION: To Terra Cotta from Toronto, take Highway 10 north to Regional Road 9 (King Street), turn west and go 8 km (5 miles), then in town turn north on Winston Churchill Boulevard and go 0.5 km (0.3 miles) to the trail intersection. Road shoulder parking is limited, but roomier on the east side. In Palgrave, on Highway 50 about 3 km (2 miles) south of Highway 9, turn east on either of the town's two major streets and go one concession to Mt. Hope Road and turn left. Parking is available at the Palgrave Ballpark on the right-hand side.

TRAIL MAP: Available through the Land Manager.

ADMISSION: Free

REPAIR SHOP: Caledon Hills Cycling Shop, 15640 McLaughlin Road, Inglewood, 905-838-1698.

TOURISM INFORMATION: Headwaters Country Tourism Association, 800-332-9744 or 519-941-1940, fax 519-942-4066.

LAND MANAGER: Town of Caledon, Parks and Recreation, 905-584-2272.

GROUP RIDES: Caledon Cycle Club, 905-838-1698.

Kolapore Uplands

Kelso Conservation Area ⑦

Ratings

LENGTH: 13 km (8 miles)

TRAIL: Singletrack

SURFACE: Clay-based hardpack with mud holes

TECHNICAL: Moderate

LAYOUT: Branching network

TOPOGRAPHY: Hardwood forest and fields on the Niagara Escarpment

AESTHETICS: Scenic view of countryside and Escarpment

IMPRESSION: Always relishable

As one of Ontario's first mountain biking hot spots, Kelso has become a classic. Everyone seems to know and love this site. The Fat Tire Festival, held annually since 1985, now attracts more than 1,000 participants for both downhill and cross-country events. Tuesday and Wednesday night race series draw about 70 riders. And daily, its parking lot is lined with cars sporting bike racks.

Kelso features a nest of singletrack trails that branch and intersect through high woods and low fields. Pick a path and turn on a whim. Have fun, get lost. Property lines and side roads will keep you in-bounds.

Wide trails bob among trees over roots, rocks, logs, and limestone outcrops. Technically they're engaging though not terribly tough. In due course, they plunge, fast and furious into fields where trails are tight streaks through agricultural crops.

The network lies behind Glen Eden Ski Area at the top of the Niagara Escarpment. The access, however, lies at the base of the ski area at the bottom of the Escarpment. That difference translates to an initial grueling, long, steep climb up loose, rocky doubletrack. A view of surrounding countryside awaits, and — of course — you can look forward to finishing with an exhilarating downhill.

Status

RESTRICTIONS: Sections of the white-blazed Bruce Trail — which runs through the park — are prohibited to bikes. Also closed are trails that run along the Escarpment's cliff edge where 1,000-year-old cedars cling to limestone rocks, and trails around the Lime Kiln Ruins in the far west corner. Riding in spring, or after heavy rains, is not permitted; call for conditions.

EVENTS: Fat Tire Festival, in spring, is organized by WOW Mountain Bike, 905-567-7593. 12-Hour Adrenaline is presented by Trilife Sports, 905-944-9436. Race series: Tuesday, presented by Spokes 'n' Slopes, 905-876-7676; Wednesday, presented by Silent Sports, 905-889-3772.

CAUTIONS: Trails tend to be two-way and heavily used by hikers on weekends.

Guide Notes

NEAREST COMMUNITY: Milton, Campbellville

LOCATION: From Highway 401 west of Toronto, take Highway 25 north (Exit 320) to Campbellville Road, go west to Tremaine Road, south to Kelso Road, west to park entrance. From the QEW take Highway 25 north (Exit 111) to Derry Road, go west to Tremaine Road, north to Kelso Road, west to park entrance. To access trails, bike through the bridge under the railway tracks up to the ski chalet and follow the maintenance road to the left.

TRAIL MAPS: Available at the Gatehouse.

FACILITIES: Bike wash, washrooms, snackbar, open limited hours. Manmade lake with a beach, canoe, kayak and windsurf rentals, organized group camping, children's playground, the Halton Region Museum and Farm Museum.

ADMISSION: $3.25 adults; annual passes available. Tags must be displayed on bikes. Open summer through fall.

TIPS: Parked cars on nearby roadways are ticketed. The park is in close biking range to Hilton Falls Conservation Area.

REPAIR SHOP: Spokes 'n' Slopes, 89 Ontario Street N. (Highway 25), Milton, 905-876-7676. Bicycle Works, 316 Dundas Street E. (Highway 5), Waterdown, 905-689-1991.

TOURISM INFORMATION: Milton Chamber of Commerce, 905-878-0581, fax 905-878-4972.

LAND MANAGER: Halton Region Conservation Authority, 905-878-5011, fax 905-878-1619, e-mail gleneden@hrca.on.ca

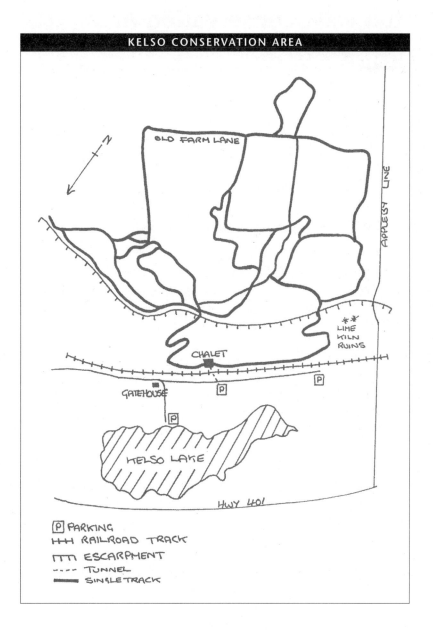

P PARKING
⊦⊦⊦ RAILROAD TRACK
ᒣᒣᒣ ESCARPMENT
- - - - TUNNEL
▬▬▬ SINGLE TRACK

Hilton Falls Conservation Area ⑧

| ● ■ ▪ | WEST OF MILTON |

Ratings

LENGTH: 15.5 km (10 miles)

TRAIL: Doubletrack and singletrack

SURFACE: Hardpacked

TECHNICAL: Easy to moderate

LAYOUT: Three linked loops, mapped and well-marked

TOPOGRAPHY: Gently rolling, hardwood forest, wetland

AESTHETICS: A waterfall, a reservoir, beaver dams, wildflowers, birds, and butterflies

IMPRESSION: Nature jaunt

Situated on the Niagara Escarpment with two tributaries of the Sixteen Mile Creek running through it, Hilton Falls Conservation Area is a pretty place with mostly smooth, wide trails.

There are 15.5 km (10 miles) of track in three loops, all canopied in mixed forest. One loop leads to a waterfall, another up a ridge and around a reservoir, the third past beaver dams and wetland. Only the latter, the Beaver Dam Trail, has technical terrain with roots, rocks and logs in its far reaches.

The waterfall — Hilton Falls — is a wide veil with a 10-meter (33 foot) drop over the Niagara Escarpment. Beside the falls stands the ruins of a mill from the mid-1800s, and downstream lies a 12,000-year-old geological pothole. Among other wildlife, the park is one of the largest breeding sites in North America for the endangered West Virginia white butterfly.

Status

POLITICS: Trails are multi-use, used by equestrians, well frequented by hikers on weekends and used by cross-country skiers in winter. The park may close to bikes during unsuitable weather.

RESTRICTIONS: Biking is not permitted on the white-blazed Bruce Trail, which runs through the southeast corner of the park, and on the Bruce's blue-blazed side trails — except those that overlap on park trails, blazed blue and yellow, or orange or red.

CAUTIONS: Log bridges are slippery when wet. Poison ivy is common on the Beaver Dam Trail. Sections are soggy in spring.

Guide Notes

NEAREST COMMUNITY: Milton, Campbellville

LOCATION: From Highway 401 west of Toronto, take Highway 25 north to Regional Road 9 and go west 6 km (4 miles). From the QEW, take Guelph Line north through Campbellville to Regional Road 9 and go east for 4 km (2.5 miles).

TRAIL MAP: Available at the Gatehouse.

FACILITIES: Visitor Centre, barbecue fire rings, washrooms

ADMISSION: $3.25 for adults; tags for bikes must be displayed. Open mid-April to the end of November. Gates close at sunset; night biking not permitted.

TIPS: The park is in close biking range to Kelso Conservation Area.

REPAIR SHOP: Spokes 'n' Slopes, 89 Ontario Street N. (Highway 25), Milton, 905-876-7676. Bicycle Works, 316 Dundas Street E. (Highway 5), Waterdown, 905-689-1991.

TOURISM INFORMATION: Milton Chamber of Commerce, 905-878-0581, fax 905-878-4972.

LAND MANAGER: Halton Region Conservation Authority, 905-854-0262 weekends, 905-336-1158 weekdays.

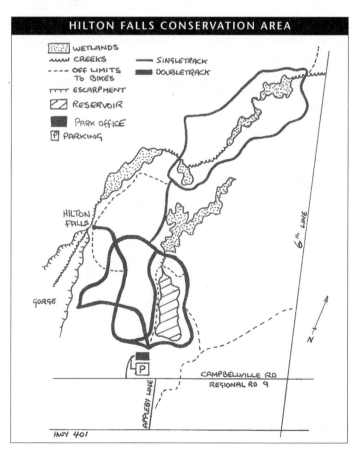

Elora Cataract Trailway

Ratings

LENGTH: 47 km (29 miles)

TRAIL: Rail trail, doubletrack

SURFACE: Resurfaced stone dust sections and original rail bed with loose, stony patches

TECHNICAL: Easy

LAYOUT: Level corridor

TOPOGRAPHY: Fields, farms, woodlands, meadows, wetlands

AESTHETICS: Diverse scenery, Shand Dam, Kettle Lakes, and spring trilliums on hillsides

IMPRESSION: A long-distance accomplishment

The Elora Cataract Trailway is a 47-km (29 mile) recreational corridor that links half a dozen towns and travels through changing countryside.

From Elora east to the hamlet of Cataract (north of Belfountain), the rail

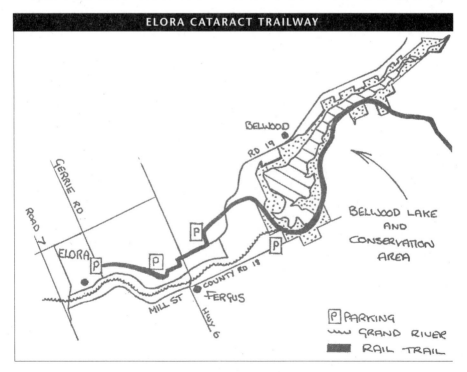

ELORA CATARACT TRAILWAY

trail cuts through farmland, mature hardwood forest, wetlands, meadows, rolling pastures and woodlots. Occasional benches among maples, beech and oak welcome sitting. Distance markers let you peel off the kilometers as you go. And most of the towns along the way have convenient trailside stores.

The scenery, while diverse, unfolds subtly, almost seamlessly between urban, rural and natural environments. The only abrupt site is the monster concrete wall of Shand Dam at Belwood Lake Conservation Area. Separating the lake from the Grand River with a 23-meter (75 foot) drop, the dam is a high perch with a great view.

The west end, from Elora to Belwood, has been resurfaced with stone dust into a smooth, wide, flat laneway suitable for children. At Fergus, however, this 16-km (10 mile) stretch is interrupted when the right-of-way comes to a dead end, makes vague reappearances, and leaves you hanging on a missing bridge. Signs detour travelers on roads, but it's possible to trace the old rail line through much of the town.

The east end from Mississauga Road to Hillsburgh — a 10-km (6 mile) stretch — has also been resurfaced with stone dust, while the middle section has loose, stony patches on original rail bed.

Now part of the Trans Canada Trail, this right-of-way was built in 1879 by the Credit Valley Railway Company as a branch of the Toronto to Orangeville mainline.

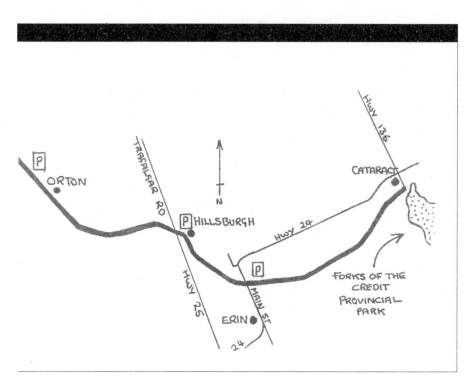

Trail map courtesy of the Elora Cataract Trailway Association

Status

POLITICS: Owned by Credit Valley and Grand River conservation authorities, the multi-use rail trail is also managed by The Elora Cataract Trailway Association, a community group. Maintenance: The Elora Cataract Trailway Association appreciates donations. Trail memberships are available for $20.

MAINTENANCE: Membership in the Elora Cataract Trailway Association, for $20, helps support the on-going maintenance work.

CAUTIONS: Some road crossings have heavy traffic.

Guide Notes

NEAREST COMMUNITIES: Belfountain, Cataract, Erin, Hillsburgh, Orton, Fergus, and Elora.

LOCATION: In Elora, at the bridge, go east on Mill Street (County Road 18) for 1.7 km (1 mile), just past Elora Quarry Conservation Area, to Gerrie Road and turn left; the parking lot is just up the road on the right-hand side. In the east: start at Erin. While the eastern terminus is at Cataract — not marked on Ontario maps — parking is forbidden in the hamlet or at any of the trail access points. In Erin, the parking lot is on the east side of Highway 24 (Main Street) at the north end of town. From Main Street, turn right on Ross Street and follow to its end. Additional parking lots are at Hillsburgh, Orton, Belwood Lake Conservation Area and Fergus.

TRAIL MAP: A map and user's guide is available from the Land Managers.

FACILITIES: En-route towns have convenience stores and gas stations.

ADMISSION: Free

TIPS: Bring your bathing suit for a swim at the Elora Quarry. At a leisurely pace with a stop for lunch, count on four to five hours for a one-way ride. Camping is available at the Elora Gorge Conservation Area, 519-846-9742.

REPAIR SHOP: Water Street Cycleworks, 21 Water Street, Elora, 519-846-8196.

TOURISM INFORMATION: Elora Information Centre, 519-846-9841, fax 519-846-2074. Headwaters Country Tourism Association, 800-332-9744 or 519-941-1940, fax 519-942-4066.

LAND MANAGERS: Elora Cataract Trailway Association, Box 99, Fergus, Ont. N1M 2W7, 519-843-3650, fax 519-843-6907, www.trailway.org
Credit Valley Conservation Authority, 800-668-5557, fax 905-670-2210.
Grand River Conservation Authority, 519-621-2761, fax 519-621-4844.

Ganaraska Forest Centre Ski Trails ⑩

NORTH OF BOWMANVILLE

Ratings

LENGTH: 30 km (19 miles)

TRAIL: Doubletrack

SURFACE: Hardpack with sandy sections

TECHNICAL: Moderate

LAYOUT: Marked and mapped loops

TOPOGRAPHY: Forested rolling hills of the Oak Ridges Moraine

AESTHETICS: Immense forest with chance of seeing wildlife

IMPRESSION: Fast, hilly, and popular

The cross-country ski trails at Ganaraska Forest provide a user-friendly introduction to southern Ontario's largest forest. The 4,160-ha (10,400 acre) Ganaraska is laced with hundreds of kilometers of trails, but only its ski network is mapped, marked and color-coded.

Totaling 30 km (19 miles), these doubletrack trails form six stacked loops. With the exception of a few sandy patches, they are hardpacked and usually dry. Situated on the Oak Ridges Moraine, the trails present big uphills, long downhills, and grand sweeping turns. The forest is lofty with hardwoods, large ferns, and pine plantations.

Throughout this network are intersecting snowmobile trails, maintenance roads, cart tracks and singletrack trails that extend well beyond the security of the marked routes. To venture off the marked course is a risky undertaking in a wooded labyrinth. Exploration requires compass skills or a buddy familiar with the intricate web. It's also advisable to have a topographical color map that includes the layout of logging roads.

Mountain bike race organizers developed the singletrack trails. The forest hosts at least four major events each season, including the Ganaraska Grinder, which attracts up to 400 riders with its 25-km (15.5 mile) tour and 50 km (31 mile) Enduro. On most weekends at least 20 cars with bike racks line the parking lot.

Status

POLITICS: The Ganaraska Forest requires membership for use of trails, though visitors are welcome. Fees go toward trail maintenance. Hikers and equestrians frequent trails.

EVENTS: 24 Hours of Summer Solstice and Ganaraska Gear Grinder, in summer, organized by Chico Racing, 905-852-0381. Paul's Dirty Enduro, in fall, organized by Ganaraska Off Road Productions, 905-797-3246.

CAUTIONS: Don't veer off marked trails without a compass, tools, food and water. Poison ivy is abundant throughout the property. Hunting is permitted in parts of the forest during hunting season in spring and fall.

Guide Notes

NEAREST COMMUNITY: Kirby, Kendal

LOCATION: Take Highway 401 east from Toronto, Highway 35/115 north to Kirby, go east on Ganaraska Road 9 for 10 km (6 miles), then north on Cold Springs Camp Road for 4 km (2.5 miles).

TRAIL MAP: Available at the Gatehouse

FACILITIES: Outhouses and a self-serve kiosk.

ADMISSION: Visitors pay a day-use fee. Membership of $15 individuals or $25 families provides unlimited use of the forest in spring, summer, and fall.

REPAIR SHOP: Proform Cycle and Accessories, between Port Hope and Cobourg on Highway 2; 905-885-4857. Bicycles Plus, 423 Bloor Street W., Oshawa, 905-436-6040. Cycle 2001, 175 Simcoe Street, Peterborough, 705-749-3364.

TOURISM INFORMATION: Tourism Durham, 800-413-0017 or 905-723-0023.

LAND MANAGER: Forest Centre, 905-797-2721. Ganaraska Region Conservation Authority, 905-885-8173.

TOURS: Guided tours of the interior, offered by Ganaraska Off Road Productions, 905-797-3246.

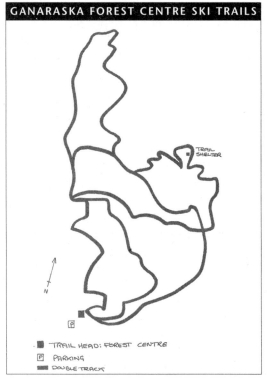

GANARASKA FOREST CENTRE SKI TRAILS

Victoria Rail Trail ⑪

KINMOUNT TO LINDSAY

Ratings

LENGTH: 55 km (34 miles)

TRAIL: Rail trail

SURFACE: Hardpack with a few crunchy gravel sections

TECHNICAL: Easy

LAYOUT: Wide, level, straight corridor

TOPOGRAPHY: Passes through urban, agricultural, rural, hamlet and natural areas

AESTHETICS: High bridges, relic cabins, juniper and rocky fields, lakeshore riding

IMPRESSION: A long, satisfying ride through changing landscape

From the restored 1874 CN railway station in the hamlet of Kinmount, the Victoria Rail Trail cuts a 55-km (34 mile), straight and level corridor south to Lindsay. Beginning on what looks like a country road, wide enough to ride side-by-side with a friend, the old rail line is a quiet streak through rural landscape.

Jack pine, red pine, poplar, maple, and tamarack keep you in a forested setting for the first half of the journey. You pedal alongside the Burnt River and over deep creeks and gorges on bridges with turquoise-colored planks made of recycled plastic. Carved passages slice through Canadian Shield Rock and raised rail bed gives way over marshes. You pass forgotten cabins and an abandoned rock quarry. Then, for a good distance, you follow the pretty, cottage-lined shore of Cameron Lake.

Fenelon Falls, 35 km (22 miles) into the journey, is a perfect lunch spot. Have a picnic at the beach or a served meal at a lock-side restaurant. To pick up the trail again, go over the bridge, south on Highway 121 (past the Tim Hortons) to the Information Chamber of Commerce in the former railway station. Turn left and go through the parking lot.

Open fields punctuated with scattered rocks, juniper bushes and cedar trees dominate the landscape. The Ken Reid Conservation Area has a wetland of bulrushes waving in a breeze on either side of the trail. It's downhill from here on a slight grade. Just before Lindsay, you'll pass between old bridge abutments from 1911.

Victoria Rail Trail

Status

POLITICS: Owned and managed by the County of Victoria, this multi-use recreational corridor is frequented by hikers and equestrians.

ETIQUETTE: Don't trespass on adjacent private property.

CAUTIONS: The majority of road crossings are quiet, but in Fenelon Falls you'll have to bike a short distance on Highway 121. Though the trail passes hamlets, it nevertheless is quite remote: be mechanically self-sufficient.

Guide Notes

NEAREST COMMUNITY: Kinmount, Fenelon Falls, Lindsay

LOCATION: To reach Kinmount from Highway 401, go north on Highway 35/115, to Highway 35. From Lindsay, go to Highway 121. Parking is available at the Tourist Information Centre at the restored CN railway station on Station Street. In Lindsay, roadside parking is available at the trail intersection. Head north into town on Highway 35 (which becomes Lindsay Street S.), turn left on Kent Street W., go one block to William Street N., turn right and go 2 km (1.2 miles). The trailhead lies between Orchard Park Road and Eglinton Street.

TRAIL MAP: Available from Victoria County Tourism.

ADMISSION: Free

TIPS: When in Kinmount, be sure to catch a movie at the Highland Cinema, 705-488-2107. The best — and only — accommodation in Kinmount is the bike-friendly Kinmount House B&B, 705-488-2421. At a leisurely pace, the route takes about five hours one-way.

REPAIR SHOP: Canadian Tire, Fenelon Falls, Highway 121, 705-887-3310. Canadian Tire, Lindsay, 377 Kent Street W, 705-324-2176.

TOURISM INFORMATION: Victoria County Tourism, 705-324-9411, fax 705-324-1750, e-mail countyvi@victourism.org www.victourism.org

LAND MANAGER: County of Victoria

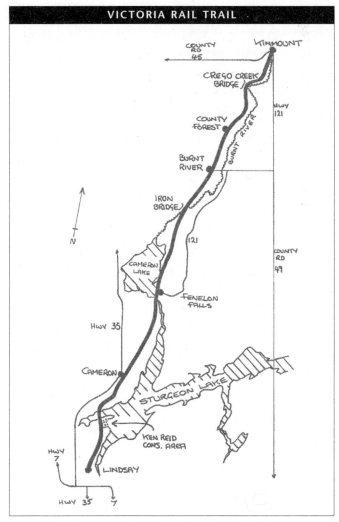

Trail map courtesy of Victoria County Tourism

Hardwood Hills Mountain Bike Centre

◉ ◼ ◆ ◆◆　NORTH OF BARRIE

Ratings

LENGTH: 70 km (43 miles)

TRAIL: Singletrack and doubletrack

SURFACE: Well-drained hardpack with sand patches and rooty sections

TECHNICAL: Easy to extreme

LAYOUT: 36 km (22 miles) of doubletrack cross-country ski trails intertwined with 45 km (28 miles) of singletrack, all well-mapped and marked

TOPOGRAPHY: Hilly forest of sugar maple and pine plantation

AESTHETICS: Outstanding fall colors

IMPRESSION: An industry standard

Ontario's most progressive mountain bike facility, Hardwood Hills features an extensive trail network, offers lessons, camps and rentals — including kids' sizes and front-suspension bikes — and has an on-site repair shop and cafeteria.

Host to many of the province's top races, including the 1997 National Championships and a 1998 Canada Cup, Hardwood is committed to the sport of mountain biking at all levels. As much as it provides elite riders with strenuous technical challenge, it gives intermediates a potent playground, and offers beginners and children gentle initiation into the off-road world.

Hardwood Hills has a dense assembly of intertwining doubletrack and singletrack trails in a 220-ha (550 acre) property of rolling forested hills. Trails are named, marked, mapped, rated, briefly described and one-way. You can plan a path before you head out, mix and match track along the way, or follow one of six preset courses.

Color-coded and used for a Wednesday night race series, the courses connect same skill-level trails. They range from the gently rolling 6-km (4 mile) Fun Course, where you can ride side-by-side on doubletrack, to the extreme 15-km (9 mile) Radical Course with severe steeps, roots, rocks, logs, and acute turns in handlebar-width tight track.

Overall, the soil is dry and well drained, but expect occasional sand patches and roots amid the hardpack.

Status

POLITICS: Privately owned, Hardwood Hills is a top-notch cross-country ski center in winter.

ETIQUETTE: Helmets required.

EVENTS: Wednesday night race series, introductory and advanced skills courses, racer development camps, kid's camps, women's camps, private lessons, maintenance courses.

MAINTENANCE: Full-time trail maintenance in summer.

CAUTIONS: Brace for sand patches. Blackflies are a nuisance in spring.

Guide Notes

NEAREST COMMUNITY: Barrie, Orillia

LOCATION: From Highway 400, stay on the Highway 400 extension north of Barrie and take Exit 111 (Doran Road.) Go east 10 km (6 miles).

TRAIL MAP: Detailed maps available on-site.

FACILITIES: Rentals, bike wash, repair shop, retail shop, cafeteria, washrooms, showers, lodging in a five-bedroom country inn (888-INN-ATHH).

ADMISSION: $7.50 adults, $3.75 children, age 7 and under free, Wednesday nights $5, season's passes available. Open daily, May to November 9 A.M. to 5 P.M., plus Wednesday 5 P.M. to dusk May to the end of August.

TIPS: Good place after a rainfall.

REPAIR SHOP: Full service on-site.

TOURISM INFORMATION: Barrie Visitor & Convention Bureau, 800-668-9100 or 705-739-9444, fax 705-739-1616.

LAND MANAGER: Hardwood Hills, 800-387-3775 or 705-487-3775, fax 705-487-2153, e-mail hardwood@bconnex.net www.hardwoodhills.on.ca

Victoria Rail Trail

North Simcoe Rail Trail ⑬

Ratings

LENGTH: 14.5 km (9 miles)

TRAIL: Rail trail

SURFACE: Original rail beds, overgrown, sandy patches

TECHNICAL: Easy

LAYOUT: Straight, wide, level corridor

TOPOGRAPHY: Farmland, swamp, and hardwood brush

AESTHETICS: Minesing Swamp, birds, and Willow Depot historical site

IMPRESSION: Interesting for those who ride slow and soak in the scenery

One third of this 15-km (9 mile) rail trail runs alongside the Minesing Swamp, one of Ontario's largest remaining wetlands, an internationally significant complex of swamps, marshes, bogs and fens. White shells from scavenged eggs litter the throughway. Birds galore squawk, chirp and flit among the reeds and bulrushes. Watch for turtles crossing the path.

The way is overgrown with grass and weeds, but the ground is nevertheless firm with the exception of a few sandy patches in the south. Moreover, overgrowth cushions the somewhat rutted and stony rail bed, making it a relatively smooth ride.

From the south, you're led through the shaded canopy of hardwood brush to an opening with a view over the Minesing Swamp and as far as Collingwood's Blue Mountains. Soon after, a ravine with dark drop-offs on either side engulfs the trail.

At approximately 4 km (2.5 miles), log steps on your right rise up an embankment to Willow Creek Depot. Stop, walk up and explore this historic site where hundreds of tons of military supplies and trade goods were stored during the War of 1812. A fort reconstruction is in the works.

A wide marsh — an excellent birding site — then surrounds the trail. It ends abruptly at a bridge crossing over Willow Creek that transfers riders into farmland, where you'll be separated from cows by an electrical fence.

The rail trail follows a portion of a railway line built in 1879 that stretched between Penetanguishene Harbour and Colwell and connected to the CN Barrie-to-Meaford line.

The few road crossings are a pain. You'll have to stop and maneuver your handlebars between narrow posts.

Status

POLITICS: North Simcoe Railtrail Inc., a non-profit charitable coalition of user groups, operates and maintains the rail trail in a lease agreement with the Springwater Township. As part of the Trans Canada Trail, improvement plans for parking lots, trail resurfacing, and facilities are underway.

ETIQUETTE: Watch for turtles. In the north you'll pass through farm property that requires you to unhook an electrical wire fence by an orange rubber handle. Be sure to replace it after you've passed through.

MAINTENANCE: Maintenance donations are appreciated; $10 sponsors a one-meter section of trail.

CAUTIONS: Poison ivy grows abundantly around the road-crossing gate north of Highway 26.

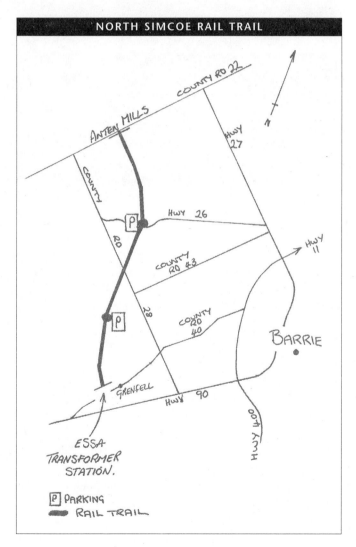

North Simcoe Rail Trail

Guide Notes

NEAREST COMMUNITY: Barrie, Midhurst, Minesing.

LOCATION: Midway on the trail is an official, but overgrown parking lot on the north side of Highway 26, 5 km (3 miles) west of Highway 27. A tall fundraising sign marks the spot. To reach the south terminus, take Highway 400 to Barrie, Highway 90 west past Highway 27, and 2.7 km (1.7 miles) past Simcoe County Road 28. Turn right on Pinegrove Road (a gravel road) and go 4 km (2.5 miles). The trail is on your right-hand side just past the railway tracks.

TRAIL MAP: A brochure with map is available through the Land Manager.

FACILITIES: Two designated parking lots, neither at the ends of the trail. Willow Creek Depot has an outhouse.

ADMISSION: Free

REPAIR SHOP: Cyclepath, 19 Dunlop Street E., Barrie, 705-726-9721. Bikeland, 49 Anne Street, Barrie, 705-726-7372.

TOURISM INFORMATION: Barrie Visitor & Convention Bureau, 800-668-9100 or 705-739-9444, fax 705-739-1616.

LAND MANAGER: North Simcoe Railtrail Inc., PO Box 272, Midhurst, Ont. L0L 1X0, 705-728-9621, e-mail trails@interhop.net

Mansfield Outdoor Centre (14)

◐ ■ ◆ ◆◆　MANSFIELD

Ratings

LENGTH: 40 km (25 miles)

TRAIL: Singletrack and doubletrack

SURFACE: Hardpack, dry and loamy

TECHNICAL: Easy to extreme

LAYOUT: Four one-way loops and one out-and-back trail, all mapped, marked, color-coded

TOPOGRAPHY: Hilly forested moraine

AESTHETICS: Groves of different tree species, a lookout

IMPRESSION: Sweet and psychotic

You want tough, brutal, radical riding? Come to Mansfield where expert trails have been designed with a little sadistic furor. Wait. Not all of Mansfield is technical — half of its 40-km (25 mile) network traces doubletrack, cross-country ski trails.

Moreover, the Wolverine, an intermediate/advanced-rated singletrack, rambles merrily among wide gaps of trees, through ravines and along the crest of ridges. Even the Achilles, an advanced/expert trail has a soft side in the east, where it weaves among pines and leads to a lookout over the Pine River Valley.

But for hardcore riders, tough trails feature tight twists through dense forest, tricky switchbacks, drop-offs, and barely climbable descents. If you're not riding precise, you're walking or smacking trees and doing endos. The margin between handlebars and trunks is often no greater than 6 cm (2 inches). The west end particularly is unforgiving, even among trail options. A fork on the Achilles, for example, offers left and right alternatives down a gully — respectively signed Crazy and Suicide. Your pick. Love it or hate it.

Mansfield Outdoor Centre offers four one-way loops; a handful of no-name interconnecting trails, plus a flat, out-and-back streak along the base of the ridge. The loops roam the top of a hilly moraine and accordingly begin with a really long climb and finish with a screamingly long descent. They all start and end from the same home base, but you needn't feel committed to any one trail; tracks merge for stretches and cross each other at various points.

Throughout, the forest is light and airy with an assortment of birch, pine, oak and maple. Leaves are everywhere: on chest-high saplings, on overhead branches, in the foreground, backdrop and on the ground — covering holes and gathering in your brake pads. The soil, a mix of sand and gravel, has excellent drainage, so trails are always dry.

Status

POLITICS: Mansfield Outdoor Centre is also a cross-country ski and outdoor education center.

EVENTS: Various races presented by WOW Mountain Bike, 905-567-7593. Also, the Centre runs a weekly race series, a residential kid's camp and men and women's clinics.

CAUTIONS: Trail markers are color-coded arrows on white plastic pointing the direction of one-way trails — not to be confused with the cross-country ski markers which are colored circles with arrows.

Mansfield Outdoor Centre

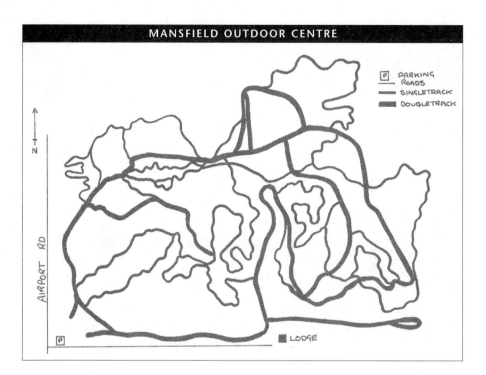

MANSFIELD OUTDOOR CENTRE

Legend: P PARKING / ROADS / SINGLETRACK / DOUBLETRACK

N

AIRPORT RD

P

P LODGE

Guide Notes

NEAREST COMMUNITY: Mansfield

LOCATION: From Highway 400, take Highway 89 west past Alliston and Rosemont, turn north on Dufferin Road 18 (Airport Road), go 10 km (6 miles).

TRAIL MAP: Available on-site.

FACILITIES: Washrooms, bike wash, snacks, drinks, limited bike and helmet rentals. On-site tenting, full-service trailer hook-ups; basic cabin rentals for groups of 25 or more.

ADMISSION: $7 adults, $3 children, $18 families; season's passes available. Open weekends and holiday Mondays only.

TIPS: Good place after a rainfall.

REPAIR SHOP: Limited services on-site. John's Cycle, 90 John Street, Orangeville, 519-941-4417.

TOURISM INFORMATION: Headwaters Country Tourism Association, 800-332-9744 or 519-941-1940, fax 519-942-4066.

LAND MANAGER: Mansfield Outdoor Centre, 705-435-4479, e-mail mansfield@sympatico.ca www.mansfield-outdoors.com

Kolapore Uplands

15

◆◆◆ SOUTHWEST OF COLLINGWOOD

Ratings

LENGTH: 50 km (31 miles)

TRAIL: Singletrack

SURFACE: Hardpack with imbedded rocks, protruding roots

TECHNICAL: Moderate to extreme

LAYOUT: Marked and mapped network

TOPOGRAPHY: Hardwood forest, outliers of the Niagara Escarpment

AESTHETICS: Semi-wilderness, leafy canopy, wildlife, vistas

IMPRESSION: Rock 'n' roll heaven

It's hard to believe these are cross-country ski trails. They're not wide, smooth, level or straight. They resemble rugged hiking trails — like sections of the Bruce Trail on the Niagara Escarpment. Indeed, Kolapore Uplands neighbors the grandaddy ridge and certain trails lead up to outlying Escarpment outcrops.

Riddled with roots and rocks, trails meander through hardwood forest, into valleys, over boardwalks at stream crossings, and up slopes to high points. A mass assortment of interconnected loops, the network is huge, the vistas are grand, and the way is challenging. The hardpacked earth is laced with imbedded rocks and protruding roots. It's bumpy, it's real, it's natural. And delightfully bike-able, regardless. Just don't plan to go fast.

The forest is bright, airy and see-through. You can see what lies ahead and to either side. Stop for a second to hear birds galore. Trilliums deck the ground in spring. The fall display of colors is spectacular.

Trails are marked with orange triangles and intersections are marked by yellow squares with numbers that correspond to numbers on the cross-country ski map. The map also rates the difficulty levels of the trails.

Status

POLITICS: The trails of Kolapore Uplands lie mostly on Crown land, but have been developed and maintained as a cross-country ski network by the University of Toronto Outing Club. Members and other volunteers devote thousands of hours constructing trails, erecting signs, building bridges, mapping and measuring trails, and clearing deadfall and new growth. Mountain bikers are urged to play a part in sweat equity or with a monetary donation. Already, mountain bikers have fixed the wet and muddy trail opening, diverting water drainage and resurfacing a 75-metre (250 foot) section. Due to the popularity of mountain biking at this property, the Ministry of Natural Resources is considering reviewing its impact.

Kolapore Uplands

RESTRICTIONS: Keep off trail sections marked on the map as "Winter Use Only." Don't ride for at least 24 hours after a rainfall.

ETIQUETTE: Comply with the entrance Mountain Bike Code and walk bikes over corduroy and wet areas; bike only between May 1 and December 1, only when dry; and stay off trails marked "environmentally sensitive."

MAINTENANCE: Maintenance days are posted at the trailhead.

CAUTIONS: Bring a full repair kit and know how to use it. Rocks are slippery when wet. Don't ride without a map.

Guide Notes

NEAREST COMMUNITY: Thornbury, Collingwood

LOCATION: Take Highway 10 north through Orangeville to Highway 24 north to Singhampton, turn left on Highway 4, then right on Grey Road 2. Continue past Feversham to Kolapore. The trails start on the left side of the road across from the gravel parking lot.

TRAIL MAP: Available from Ravenna General Store, 5 km north of Kolapore on Grey Road 2; sale proceeds go towards trail maintenance.

FACILITIES: Parking lot

ADMISSION: Free

REPAIR SHOP: Jolleys Cycle Centre, Highway 26, 2 km west of Meaford on the south side; 519-538-3000.

TOURISM INFORMATION: Beaver Valley Chamber of Commerce, 519-599-5724.

LAND MANAGER: Ministry of Natural Resources, Owen Sound, 519-376-3860.

Ontario

WEST

Guelph Lake

Ted's Range Road Diner

16

■ ▪ ◆ ◆◆ NORTHWEST OF MEAFORD

Ratings

LENGTH: 8 km (5 miles)

TRAIL: Singletrack with a doubletrack opener

SURFACE: Bumpy hardpack

TECHNICAL: Hard to extreme

LAYOUT: Unmapped, unmarked loop with joiners

TOPOGRAPHY: Hardwood forest, creek crossings

AESTHETICS: Hidden woods, party diner

IMPRESSION: Diamond in the rough

First, the ambiance. Ted's Range Road Diner is an establishment in the middle of nowhere overlooking Nottawasaga Bay. The place is not elegant. A small metal aircraft hanger larger on the inside than it appears from the outside is filled with wooden tables, a bar with stools, and a stage. Every Wednesday night a full-fledged party erupts to live music. Rock guitarist Kim Mitchell played here. Owen Sounders drive 40 minutes for good country cooking.

So what's this got to do with mountain biking? Ted's Diner sits on the edge of a 40-ha (100 acre) property owned by Ted Lye and his wife Kate. Here's the crux: Ted is cool. When, one day a few years ago, employees from Jolleys Cycle Centre in Meaford approached him about developing mountain bike trails on his property, Ted said, "Go to it." Rakes, pruners, beads of sweat and weeks later, voila, singletrack.

What begins as a rutted, washed-out road through grassy field, leads down into a forested valley, across a creek and up onto a wooded plateau. So far, a 6-km (4 mile) loop, lightly marked with orange flagging tape, as well as a couple of vague joiner trails, have been developed. The potential of this site is awesome.

Already, the site has been host to a race, but trails have yet to be worn smooth. The ride is tight and bumpy with off-camber meanders, narrow ravines, scary hills and steep ascents.

The forested valley is a mess of thin trees while the wooded plateau features mature forest and open areas on a wildly zigzagging course. The creek crossing is on rocks, and ravines are bridged roughly with logs.

Status

POLITICS: Ted's Range Road Diner is privately owned land with mountain bike riding approval.

ETIQUETTE: After riding, buy a cold one from Ted's in appreciation for the land use.

EVENTS: Keep tuned to Jolleys.

MAINTENANCE: Employees at Jolleys voluntarily develop and maintain trails as their time permits.

CAUTIONS: For most part there's good drainage, but a few slopes of clay make slippery, not-quick-to-dry, slides.

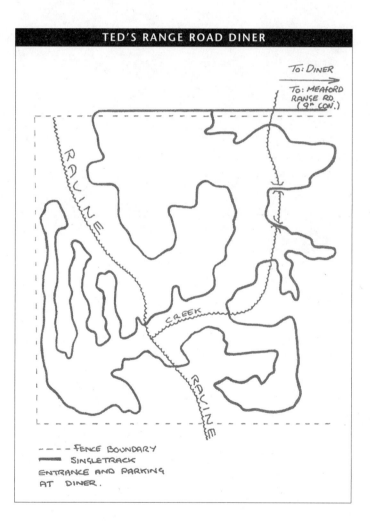

Ted's Range Road Diner

Guide Notes

NEAREST COMMUNITY: Meaford

LOCATION: From Highway 26 west of Meaford, go north on Meaford Range Road (9th Concession) 2.8 km. Ted's Diner is on the left; trails lie behind it.

TRAIL MAP: Not available.

FACILITIES: Parking, restaurant, and bar

ADMISSION: Free. The Diner is closed Tuesday afternoons. Mountain biking is not allowed during paintball games, held monthly on the property.

TIPS: Get initiated to the network with someone who knows it.

SHOP: Jolleys Cycle Centre, Highway 26, 2 km west of Meaford on the south side; 519-538-3000, fax 519-538-2734.

TOURISM INFORMATION: Meaford Chamber of Commerce, 519-538-1640, fax 519-538-5240 www.meaford.com

LAND OWNER: Ted Lye, 519-538-1788.

GROUP RIDES: Contact Jolleys.

Inglis Falls Conservation Area ⑰

Ratings

LENGTH: 12 km (7.5 miles)

TRAIL: Wide singletrack and groomed path

SURFACE: Hardpack and crushed limestone

TECHNICAL: Three separate levels: very easy, moderate and extreme

LAYOUT: Upper forest and lower parkland linked by a traverse down the Niagara Escarpment

TOPOGRAPHY: Forested Niagara Escarpment, manicured parkland

AESTHETICS: A waterfall, ferns, birds, wildflowers, orchids, and a riverside meander

IMPRESSION: A mellow ride in a beautiful setting

Inglis Falls Conservation Area, famous for its 18-meter (59 foot) waterfall, consists of three parts: a singletrack loop through rich forest, a technical descent down the Niagara Escarpment, and an easy riverside meander through parkland.

The 3-km (2 mile) singletrack loop, which begins from the parking lot on the Escarpment, is wide, well worn and playful with swooping dips, occasional roots and outcrops of rock. The forest, a healthy mix of high deciduous and coniferous trees, features one of the finest fern habitats in Ontario, with close to 30 varieties. Roll slowly, soak in the scenery; the park also has 40 different species of orchids and an abundance of wildflowers.

Near the loop's end, you'll be given a choice of two ways down the Escarpment: steep and very steep. Either way presents a tricky glut of embedded rocks jutting at rude angles. For most of us, this is a hike-a-bike descent.

At the bottom you're back on wide singletrack, riding on the embankment of the Sydenham River over a slew of well-built bridges. Salmon, rainbow and brown trout can be seen in the rapids each spring and fall. The trail then shifts into a clearing between high grass and farm fields before veering back into the woods.

Next, it's downhill to Mile Drive, a broken, pot-holed, former road that leads down to a parking lot and into Harrison Park, a 40-ha (100 acre), rectangular jewel of green space in the city center of Owen Sound. The trail here is smooth and level, surfaced with crushed limestone.

Status

POLITICS: Inglis Falls is the only conservation area within the Grey Sauble Conservation Authority where mountain biking is permitted. Hikers frequent trails.

ETIQUETTE: Stick to the trail.

CAUTIONS: Trails have two-way traffic. The trail map doesn't correspond to en-route signposts, but signposts deliver.

Inglis Falls Conservation Area

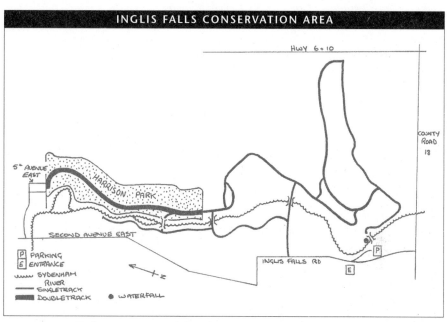

Trail map courtesy of the Grey Sauble Conservation Authority

Guide Notes

NEAREST COMMUNITY: Owen Sound

LOCATION: From Highway 6/10 south of Owen Sound, turn west at Rockford onto County Road 18, then right on Inglis Falls Road. The entrance is on your right-hand side.

TRAIL MAP: Available at the on-site gift shop.

FACILITIES: Inglis Falls is a day-use park with outhouses, a gift shop, and picnic pavilion. Harrison Park offers camping, swimming, paddleboats, canoes, and has a bird sanctuary, snack bar, and restaurant.

ADMISSION: Free

TIPS: Rumor has it the food is good at the restaurant in Harrison Park. Camping at Harrison Park Family Campground, 519-371-9734, and at Kelso Beach Campground, 519-376-1440.

REPAIR SHOP: Earl Georgas Ski & Summer Sports Shop, 132 9th Street E., 519-376-1315. Garb & Gear Source for Sports, 1063 2nd Avenue E., and 519-376-5555. Terry's Cycle & Repair Shop, 101 10th Street E., 519-376-0766.

TOURISM INFORMATION: Owen Sound Tourism, 888-675-5555 or 519-371-9833, fax 519-371-8628, e-mail vacation@city.owen-sound.on.ca www.city.owen-sound.on.ca

LAND MANAGER: Grey Sauble Conservation Authority, 519-376-3076.

MacGregor Point Provincial Park ⑱

Ratings

LENGTH: 15 km (9 miles)

TRAIL: Wide groomed singletrack and doubletrack

SURFACE: Hardpack, gravel, and sandy patches

TECHNICAL: Easy

LAYOUT: Four trails, marked and mapped

TOPOGRAPHY: Flat, lakeshore, wetland, woodland

AESTHETICS: Beaches, coves, marshes, birdlife, camping, swimming and sunsets

IMPRESSION: Ideal family mountain biking and camping destination

MacGregor Point is one in a mere handful of provincial parks that allow mountain biking. Of its 100,000 seasonal visitors, 35 percent take advantage of this opportunity to ride. Of the park's five trails, only one is off-limits. The park requires that mountain bikers walk across boardwalks.

Hugging the shore of Lake Huron, the park is a mix of wetlands, woodlands, beach ridges, sand dunes and coves. A shoreline trail stretches the length of the park. A wetland trail skirts a huge marsh. A singletrack links the two, and a boundary township road completes a loop. In addition, there's a short, former access road for bikes-only through hardwoods brush.

The 6-km (4 mile) blue-blazed Old Shore Road Trail runs under the shade of cedars, with intermittent views of the lake. The former settlement road between Goderich and Southampton is now a wide, firm track with links to all the campground areas, and access to all the rocky coves and sandy beaches. Rumor has it that the southernmost, least-visited beach is swimsuit optional.

The Ducks Unlimited Trail runs alongside a reflooded wetland — thanks to Ducks Unlimited — an observation tower and along a dike. Expect to see great blue herons and ducks galore. Sightings of beaver, muskrat and painted turtles are also common. The trail is smooth with hardpack and crushed gravel, while the dike is a bumpy doubletrack.

Status

POLITICS: MacGregor Point is one of less than half a dozen provincial parks to allow mountain biking. Hikers often use the bike trails.

RESTRICTIONS: Don't ride on the boardwalks; walk your bike. Stay off hiking-only trails.

ETIQUETTE: Ride slow.

Guide Notes

NEAREST COMMUNITY: Port Elgin

LOCATION: Located 6 km (4 miles) south of Port Elgin and 30 km (18.5 miles) north of Kincardine, follow signs off Highway 21.

TRAIL MAP: Available at the Gatehouse and Visitor's Centre.

FACILITIES: Bike rentals, camping, yurt accommodation, swimming, interpretive programs, playground, reservations.

ADMISSION: $7.50 day use

TIPS: Reserve in advance for weekend campsites. Watch the sunset.

REPAIR SHOP: Cycle Source, 522B Goderich Street, Port Elgin, 519-389-4411. MFM, 616 Goderich Street, Port Elgin, 519-389-3791. Rick's Bikes, 761 Goderich Street, Port Elgin, and 519-832-2744. Thorncrest Outfitters, 193 High Street, Southampton, 519-797-1608.

TOURISM INFORMATION: Port Elgin Chamber of Commerce, 800-387-3456 or 519-832-2332, fax 519-389-3725.

LAND MANAGER: MacGregor Point Provincial Park, 519-389-9056, fax 519-389-9057, www.ontparks.com

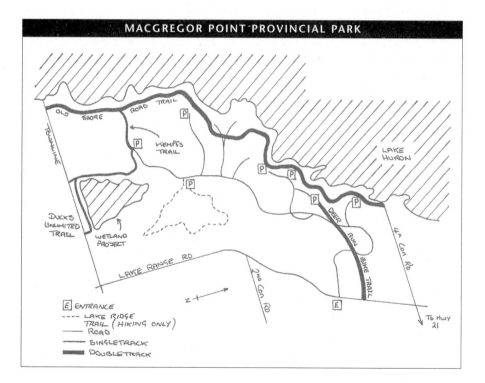

Guelph Lake (19)

 GUELPH, NORTHEAST END

Ratings

LENGTH: 10 km (6 miles)

TRAIL: Singletrack

SURFACE: Well-worn, hardpacked with good drainage

TECHNICAL: Moderate to hard

LAYOUT: Unmarked, somewhat blazed, looped network

TOPOGRAPHY: Forest and fields with steep little hills

AESTHETICS: Different forest patches, wildflowers, Guelph Lake

IMPRESSION: Intensely diverse

Weaving a maze through extremely diverse terrain, the trails of Guelph Lake are highly entertaining. The trail first skirts a farmer's field, soon dances among cedar, then streaks through a tunnel of pine.

In the ever-changing landscape, trails branch and corkscrew among trunks, wind through fields and lead to a dike on Guelph Lake. Roots, rocks, steep little dips and climbs, larger undulations, slope traverses, a natural half-pipe, and old rock-pile property lines keep you constantly on guard.

The 10-km (6 mile) network is the creation of GORBA, the Guelph Off-Road Bicycling Association. The advocacy group was formed in 1992 when the Grand River Conservation Authority granted permission for multi-use trail development on a chunk of land between Guelph Lake and a marsh.

Main trails are blazed yellow and pink, but the network can nevertheless have you spinning in circles. There are plans to color-code and name various loops, but until that becomes a reality, expect to get disoriented or aim to join GORBA on its monthly group initiation tours.

Status

POLITICS: GORBA develops and maintains the trails and runs a mountain bike patrol on the network.

ETIQUETTE: Respect trail closures and private property.

EVENTS: Numerous races, events, group rides.

MAINTENANCE: Steep embankments have been reinforced with cedar rails and rocks. Water erosion points have been averted with the placement of collapsible waterbars. Grunt work is done by volunteers the second Saturday of every month except in July. Maintenance equipment is paid for with membership fees.

Guelph Lake

CAUTIONS: Most riders park on the shoulder of Victoria Road North, just south of the Speed River bridge. It's a busy road and not a safe place to stop and unload. Park instead at Riverside Park and ride the Royal Recreation Trail to Victoria Road North and the Guelph Lake trailhead — directly across the road. Cross carefully.

Guide Notes

NEAREST COMMUNITY: Guelph

LOCATION: To Riverside Park from Highway 401, take Highway 6 North (Hanlon Expressway) to Speedvale Avenue and turn right. At Woolwich Street turn left, at Marilyn Drive, turn right. Park in the lot and ride north 3.4 km (2 miles) alongside the Speed River to the trailhead on the other side of Victoria Road North.

TRAIL MAP/INFORMATION: Maps not available; the one shown here is a rough outline; not all spurs and links are indicated. For information contact GORBA.

FACILITIES: None

ADMISSION: Free

TIPS: Get initiated with GORBA's monthly group ride.

REPAIR SHOP: Revolutions Bicycle, 43 Cork Street E., 519-766-4082.

TOURISM INFORMATION: Guelph Visitor & Convention Services, 519-837-1335, fax 519-837-1527, e-mail visitinfo@city.guelph.on.ca www.city.guelph.on.ca

LAND MANAGER: Grand River Conservation Authority, 519-621-2761, fax 519-621-4844.

CLUB/GROUP RIDES: GORBA runs group rides on the first Sunday of every month beginning from the bandshell at Riverside Park at 11 A.M., also night rides, races, events. Annual membership $20. Hotline: 519-821-8013.

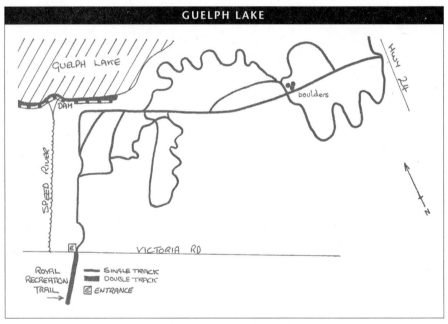

Trail map courtesy of GORBA

Dundas Valley Conservation Area (20)

Ratings

LENGTH: 58 km (36 miles)

TRAIL: Wide singletrack, grassy corridors, reconditioned gravel sections

SURFACE: Main trails are gravel, minor trails are clay-based hardpack with few roots and rocks

TECHNICAL: Moderate

LAYOUT: 40-km network of 5 main doubletrack trails and 10 minor singletrack trails and an 18-km (11 mile) rail trail

TOPOGRAPHY: Hilly, heavily wooded, primarily deciduous surrounded by the Niagara Escarpment

AESTHETICS: Views, waterfalls, spring wildflowers, beautiful fall foliage, a variety of settings, historic sites

IMPRESSION: Extremely scenic, extensive, intermediate territory

Dundas Valley Conservation Area is huge, hilly, surrounded by the heavily wooded Niagara Escarpment. Its trails are hardpacked, wide singletrack mostly, with little technical riding but tough climbs with long descents.

The area includes many settings. Follow a creek, coast down deep dells, pedal to high points, across meadows, through lush valleys and fields of berry bushes; along ridges, ravines, past cliffs, to the tops of waterfalls and to plateaus of rock. See the Hermitage, the remains of a commanding stone mansion, or visit the Griffin House, the former home of an African-American slave that escaped on the Underground Railroad.

Besides its 40-km (25 mile) network of main and minor trails, Dundas Valley encompasses an 18-km (11 mile) rail trail stretching from Hamilton to Jerseyville. It is the eastern half of the Hamilton-to-Brantford Rail Trail (included separately in this book). Moreover, this conservation area is one of the few spots where riding is allowed on the Bruce Trail, the 750-km (465 mile) hiking trail that traces the Niagara Escarpment.

The park is complex with a collage of properties, partitioned by roads and laced with myriad trails that have left visitors lost and confused — even with a map in hand. At the time of publication, however, park management was streamlining, re-marking and re-mapping its network. A loop was created in the park's center, from the replica railway station that serves as a Trail Centre. From it, four color-coded, gravel doubletrack access trails radiate north, south, east and west. Looped minor, singletrack trails branch from these lines, marked with logos on posts.

Status

POLITICS: Mountain bikers have no restrictions, but the impact of trail riding is being monitored. A few years ago, the sheer high volume of bikers, their high speeds, conflicts with other trail users and the creation of illegal new trails had park officials posting speed limits and considering a variety of restrictions. But thanks to a group of volunteer patrollers of various user-groups — including the Hamilton-Wentworth Mountain Bike Association — riders are more respectful.

RESTRICTIONS: Park closes at sunset. If you're not out, a search and rescue party will look for you. Do not create new trails. Do not ride when it's wet. The Bruce Trail, outside of Dundas Valley, is prohibited to mountain bikes.

ETIQUETTE: Ride at a moderate speed. Ride only marked trails and ignore unsigned trails. If you ride on weekends, Saturday tends to be less busy than Sunday. Winter riding is not encouraged.

EVENTS: Celebrate the Valley, with group rides and a skills clinic, among other events, takes place each spring; contact the Land Manager.

MAINTENANCE: Your volunteer efforts for various projects with the Hamilton Wentworth Mountain Bike Association are much appreciated, 905-664-6500, e-mail daveseto@idirect.com.

CAUTIONS: Remain vigilant for other trail users. If caught in the rain, ride carefully; trails are slippery when wet.

Guide Notes

NEAREST COMMUNITY: Dundas, Ancaster, and Hamilton

LOCATION: From the QEW, take Highway 403 to Main Street W. (a three-lane main artery) and go 2.3 km (1.5 miles) into the town of Dundas. From the "Welcome to Dundas" sign, go 1.3 km (0.8 miles) to Governor's Road (a Tim Hortons is at the intersection) and turn left. Drive 3 km (2 miles) west and watch for the Dundas Valley Conservation Area Park signs. Continue 0.5 km (0.3 miles) past the sign then turn left into the park's main entrance. A coin-operated, automatic gate ($5 in change required) provides entrance. Drive 0.5 km (0.3 miles) to the main parking lot. From here, walk up to the Trail Centre in the relic railway station to buy a map.

Alternatively, from the intersection of Highways 5, 8 and 52, go south on Highway 52 to Regional Road 299 (Governor's Road) at Copetown, turn left (east) at the flashing lights and drive 6 km (4 miles) to the second conservation sign and turn right.

TRAIL MAP/INFORMATION: *The Adventure Map to Dundas Valley*, a plastic-coated, topographical map, approximately $8, is available from the Trail Centre, weekends and holidays (905-627-1233), and also from the local bike shops and outfitters.

FACILITIES: Trail Centre with information on the vast array of plants, birds and animals that inhabit the area, also snacks, refreshments, and souvenirs.

ADMISSION: $5 per vehicle, annual passes are $75. Open year-round, the park closes at sunset.

TIPS: You'll need a map. Bring $5 in coins to enter the automatic gate. For trail conditions, 905-627-1233 ext. 1.

REPAIR SHOP: Freewheel Cycle, 9 King Street W., Dundas, 905-628-5126. Spin Cycle (it's beside a laundromat), 242 Governor's Road, 905-627-2426.

TOURISM INFORMATION: Conservation Lands of Ontario, 888-376-2212, www.conservationlands.com Greater Hamilton Tourist Information Centre, 805-263-8590 or 905-546-2666, fax 905-540-5099, www.hamilton-went.on.ca

LAND MANAGER: Hamilton Region Conservation Authority, 888-319-4722, www.hamrca.on.ca

GROUP RIDES: Sunday and Wednesday night rides to various local areas with Freewheel Cycle, 905-628-5126. Wednesday group rides with Pierik's Cycle, 840 King Street W., Hamilton, 905-525-8521.

Hamilton-to-Brantford Rail Trail

Hamilton-to-Brantford Rail Trail ㉑

WITH OPTIONAL TRAIL LINKS ALL THE WAY TO CAMBRIDGE

 HAMILTON TO BRANTFORD

Ratings

LENGTH: 32 km (20 miles)

TRAIL: Doubletracked rail trail

SURFACE: Crushed limestone, smooth

TECHNICAL: No

LAYOUT: Straight, wide corridor

TOPOGRAPHY: Forest, fields, woodlots, pastures

AESTHETICS: History and geography signposts, rural setting

IMPRESSION: Fast educational laneway; fine for pulling kid buggies

It's uphill practically the whole way, from Hamilton to Brantford on the abandoned railway. The ascent isn't steep, but it's persistent, from the depths of Dundas Valley to the heights of the Niagara Escarpment to the banks of the Grand River.

Built before the age of cars and affectionately known as the To Hell and Back, the Toronto Hamilton & Buffalo Railway (TH&B) was completed in 1885. Today, the 32-km (20 mile) converted rail trail offers a trip through time.

Near the start, Binkley Hollow features signposts with archival photographs of the trestle bridge that once spanned the huge ravine. Consider that railway workers at the time were paid 15 cents an hour, and ride on.

At the top of the Escarpment, Summit Station — one of six stations that once existed between Hamilton and Jerseyville — had a water tower where steam-powered locomotives would refuel. Historical photographs depict the building in a barren landscape, a stark contrast to the present lush surroundings. A signpost describes the Summit Bog, a former lake formed between 12,000 and 18,000 years ago when a massive block of ice broke off a glacier and melted, leaving a deep hole.

For a link between two major cities, this corridor is surprisingly pastoral. Covered with crushed limestone, the trail is wide and smooth, ideal for riding side-by-side with a friend. The return is a downhill coast, practically the whole way.

Status

POLITICS: This multi-use rail trail is part of the Trans Canada Trail. It's heavily used by hikers and joggers.

ETIQUETTE: Keep to the right-hand side, and if riding side-by-side, yield to oncoming traffic and to faster riders approaching from behind.

CAUTIONS: Road crossings, bordered with gates, require slow tight turns. Take care crossing Highway 57.

Guide Notes

NEAREST COMMUNITY: Hamilton, Jerseyville, and Brantford

LOCATION: In Hamilton, from the QEW, take Highway 403 to Main Street W. (a three-lane main artery) past McMaster University and turn left on Ewen Road, then right on Ofield Road; parking lot is on your right-hand side. In Brantford, from Highway 403, exit at Garden Avenue South, turn right on Colborne Street, left on Locks Road and right on Greenwich Street; parking lot is on your left-hand side.

TRAIL MAP: Available from the Land Managers.

FACILITIES: Parking lots at both end and in connecting cities.

ADMISSION: Free

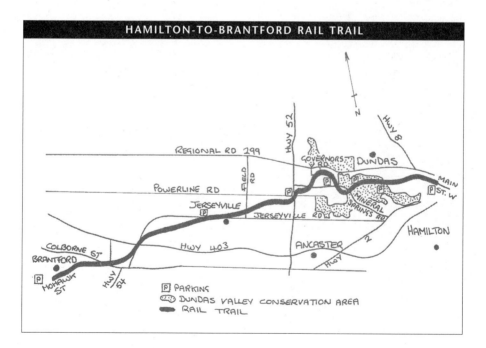

HAMILTON-TO-BRANTFORD RAIL TRAIL

TIPS: Care to carry on — all the way to Cambridge on an 80-km (50 mile) journey? Where the trail ends in Brantford, the Gordon Glaves Memorial Pathway continues. It runs to the S. C. Johnson Trail, opened in fall 1998, which stretches from Brantford to Paris and links to the Cambridge to Paris Rail trail (see Chapter). A free brochure, "Explore the Hamilton-Brantford-Cambridge Trails," produced by the Grand River Conservation Authority, provides a map with descriptive text.

REPAIR SHOP: Mountain Top Bicycles, 525 Mohawk Road E., Hamilton, 905-575-8773. Main Cycle & Sport, 1461 Main Street E., Hamilton, 905-544-0338. The Bicycle Shop, 224 Clarence Street, Brantford, 519-752-4106.

TOURISM INFORMATION: The Conservation Lands Of Ontario, 888-376-2212 or 519-621-2761. Tourism Hamilton-Wentworth, 800-263-8590 or 905-546-4222, fax 905-546-4107. Tourism Brantford, 519-751-9900.

LAND MANAGER: Grand River Conservation Authority, 519-621-2761, fax 519-621-4844. Hamilton Region Conservation Authority, 888-319-4722, www.hamrca.on.ca

Hamilton-to-Brantford Rail Trail

Cambridge-to-Paris Rail Trail

WITH OPTIONAL TRAIL LINKS ALL THE WAY TO HAMILTON

● ▮ ▮ ▮	CAMBRIDGE TO PARIS

Ratings

LENGTH: 19 km (12 miles)

TRAIL: Rail trail

SURFACE: Crushed gravel lane, smooth and dusty

TECHNICAL: No

LAYOUT: Straight, wide riverside corridor

TOPOGRAPHY: Level lane, Carolinian Forest, woods, clearings

AESTHETICS: Overlooks, relic structures, unusual southern flora, a Canadian Heritage River

IMPRESSION: A gentle ride with lovely spots, sweet for a date

Paralleling the east bank of the Grand River, the Cambridge-to-Paris Rail Trail is lined with trees, flush with wildflowers, and spotted with curious relic structures and benches at overlooks.

Tracing the old Lake Erie and Northern Electric Railway Line, the multi-use recreational corridor is an intriguing, pretty, peaceful route. Ride it slow: past wetland flush with cattails, ferns and lady-slippers; under leafy canopies where warblers and songbirds flit among branches; through clearings where turkey vultures circle overhead.

A trail brochure published by the Grand River Conservation Authority provides more subtle details. It tells where a 1996 tornado uprooted large trees, where old wooden ties and steel spikes lie hidden, and where you can fill your waterbottle from a natural spring.

Glen Morris Station, at midway, used to be the site of cattle-loading pens. Today snapping turtles lay their eggs here each June. The trees south of Glen Morris include Carolinian species from more southern climates, such as sassafras, shagbark hickory and sycamore.

One overlook features the remnants of a rare Prairie grass habitat. Ruins are identified: the huge, roofless Glen Morris Mill, a coal-powered generating station, and the tall river abutments of the 1933-abandoned CNR Toronto-to-Windsor rail line.

Near Paris, a rafting, canoeing and kayaking outfitter called Adventures-on-the-Grand offers a trailside tearoom.

Cambridge-to-Paris Rail Trail

Status

POLITICS: Opened in 1994, the Cambridge-to-Paris Rail Trail is part of the Trans Canada Trail. The trail is heavily used by hikers, birders, couples walking arm-in-arm, parents pushing baby strollers, and dogs pulling their masters.

ETIQUETTE: Ride slow and keep to the right-hand side. Stay off adjacent private property.

MAINTENANCE: Donations for continued maintenance and improvements are welcome through the Grand River Foundation at the Grand River Conservation Authority.

Guide Notes

NEAREST COMMUNITY: Cambridge, Glen Morris, and Paris

LOCATION: At the south end of Cambridge, there's a parking lot on Highway 24, 1 km south of Highway 97 next to the GTO Gas Station. In Paris, from Highway 403, take Highway 2 through the first set of lights (past Tim Hortons restaurant) onto Green Lane and turn left at the T-intersection onto Willow Street; the parking lot is 0.5 km (0.3 miles) on your right. In Glen Morris, a parking lot is at the end of Washington Street.

TRAIL MAP: Available at parking lot display boards.

FACILITIES: Parking at both ends and in the middle at Glen Morris.

ADMISSION: Free

TIPS: Care to carry on — all the way to Hamilton on an 80-km-long (50-mile-long) journey? The S. C. Johnson Trail, opened in fall 1998, offers a link from Paris to Brantford, where the Gordon Glaves Memorial Pathway links to the Hamilton-to-Brantford Rail Trail (see page 72). A free brochure, "Explore the Hamilton-Brantford-Cambridge Trails," produced by the Grand River Conservation Authority, provides a map with descriptive text.

REPAIR SHOP: Sports Excellence: 52 Grand River Street N., Paris, 519-442-6843; 653 King Street, Cambridge, 519-653-4651.

TOURISM INFORMATION: Conservation Lands of Ontario, 888-376-2212, www.conservationlands.com

LAND MANAGER: Grand River Conservation Authority, 519-621-2761.

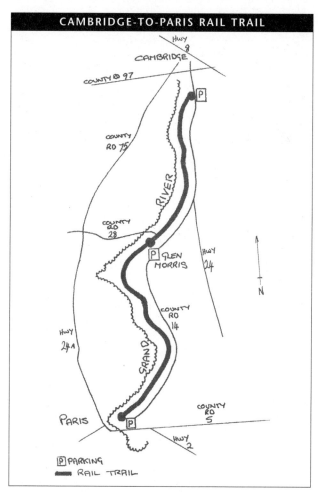

Trail map courtesy of the Grand River Conservation Authority

The Pines

23

■ □ ◆ ■ WOODSTOCK, NORTHEAST END

Ratings

LENGTH: 12 km (7.5 miles)

TRAIL: Singletrack

SURFACE: Hardpack with sandy patches, spring mud

TECHNICAL: Moderate to hard

LAYOUT: 7-km (4.5 mile) marked route, plus offshoots

TOPOGRAPHY: White pine forest, flat terrain with a few abrupt steeps

AESTHETICS: Pine corridors, open high points

IMPRESSION: Fast giant slalom turns, cool pines

Strands of white pine are the hallmark of this developed hot spot. On pine-needle-covered ground, singletrack trail corkscrews among trees with tight, banked, rhythmic turns. Blue and orange arrows mark the course: a 7-km (4.5 mile) one-way route.

Do the loop a few times and you'll know where to gear down for sudden sharp steeps, and where to gear up to ski through trees with speed. While newer trail segments and offshoots are rough and rooted, established track rides as smooth as glass. Speed is the challenge — and the thrill.

Speaking of thrill, the route blasts out of the woods onto a hill with a view — and a heck of a drop-off at about the halfway point. Go for the drop, if you're game, or take the easier ravine alternative.

The Pines has been developed by mountain bike members of the Woodstock Cycling Club. Opened in 1993, it is now host to a Tuesday night time-trial series and an annual race.

Status

POLITICS: The Woodstock Cycling Club leases the land, which is a remote part of Pittock Conservation Area, from the Upper Thames Conservation Authority. Trails were developed by fewer than half a dozen club members. Dog walkers frequent the trails.

ETIQUETTE: Follow the one-way trail signs. Respect closures; various sections are roped off when muddy and when in need of rejuvenation or repair.

EVENTS: Tuesday night time trails, annual race

MAINTENANCE: The club holds maintenance and clean-up days three times a year.

CAUTIONS: For a change of scenery, some regulars ride in the wrong direction; make yourself known on blind corners and intersections. Dirt bikes and all-terrain vehicles use the area illegally. Flies and mosquitoes are brutal in spring.

The Pines

Guide Notes

NEAREST COMMUNITY: Woodstock

LOCATION: From Highway 401, take Highway 2 east 1 km (0.6 miles), go north on County Road 4 for 4 km (2.5 miles) and turn right on Township Road 4 just before the bridge and go 0.7 km (0.4 miles). You'll see an orange trail sign on your left in the woods and just after, a little gravel shoulder where you can park.

TRAIL MAP: Not available.

FACILITIES: Limited parking. Pittock Conservation Area (519-539-5088) offers camping, swimming, boating, fishing and also has a separate 8 km (5 miles) of multi-use trails — free for use — on the south side of Pittock Lake. (To access these trails turn east on Devonshire Avenue from Highway 59, and at the first set of lights turn north on Huron Street, which ends at Roth Park and the trail parking lot.)

ADMISSION: Free, but non-club members are requested to pay an annual $5 donation. Club membership is $30.

REPAIR SHOP: Pedal Power, 590 Dundas Street, Woodstock, 519-539-3681.

TOURISM INFORMATION: Woodstock and District Chamber of Commerce, 519-539-9411, fax 519-539-5433.

LAND MANAGER: Upper Thames Conservation Authority, 519-451-2800.

CLUB: Woodstock Cycling Club, 590 Dundas Street, Woodstock, N4S 1C8; 519-539-4734, fax 519-539-3681.

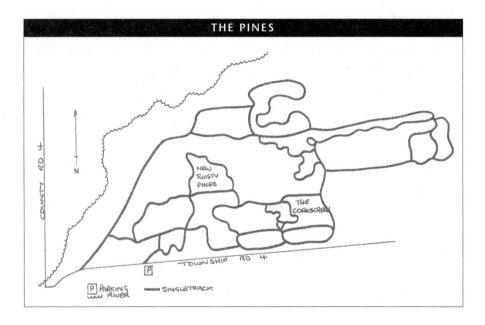

THE PINES

Boler Mountain

24

■ □ ◆   LONDON, WEST END

Ratings

LENGTH: 10 km (6 miles)

TRAIL: Singletrack

SURFACE: Hardpack with sandy loam and clay; excellent drainage

TECHNICAL: Moderate to hard

LAYOUT: Well-marked and mapped main loop with side trails

TOPOGRAPHY: Hardwood forest and fields behind a ski hill

AESTHETICS: Maples, ravines, and ground hogs

IMPRESSION: Lap it up; a fast training ground

Don't be fooled. This bike center on a ski hill is not made of downhills and slope traverses. Trails don't touch the ski area, but lace the forest behind it.

The ride starts from the base chalet with a gradual 37-meter (125 foot) climb to the hill's backside. From here, there's a well-marked, one-way loop with side trails. The main loop, marked with black arrows, presents a rollicking intermediate-level singletrack, while blue and red offshoots respectively present tougher technically invitations.

Locals grind out laps, making fast turns on banked corners, plunging down steeps that rocket back up, hopping over log obstacles and jumping off mounds. Well-maintained and broken-in, the trail is smooth and labeled. Do a few loops and you'll be talking about the Compressor, Bob's Stairway, and Luke's Labyrinth.

Given the small 48-ha (120 acre) property, the network is a tight weave that takes advantage of seemingly every ravine and oscillation. On a weekend day, when it is host to 60 riders, you'll see comrades streaking through trees on a ridge above or soaring through a ravine below. Boler has been site to Canada Cup and Ontario Cup races.

Status

POLITICS: Opened in 1995 at the London Ski Club, a public ski resort, Boler Mountain Bike Centre has grown to become London's fat-tire hot spot.

ETIQUETTE: Helmets are mandatory. Follow the one-way trail signs.

EVENTS: Weekly race series, night rides, women's rides, demo days, kid's camps, rental bike sell-off.

CAUTIONS: Two-way traffic on the edge of a field. Don't barrel down the Compressor — named for a reason — until you learn the impact of its base.

Boler Mountain

Guide Notes

NEAREST COMMUNITY: London

LOCATION: From Highway 401 take Highway 402 to Highway 4. Go north 5 km (3 miles) — past the Highway 2 intersection where Highway 4 becomes Colonel Talbot Road. Turn left on Southdale Road. Go 1 km (0.6 miles) to Boler Road, turn right, go 1 km (0.6 miles) to Griffith Street, turn left, go 1 km (0.6 miles) and follow signs.

TRAIL MAP: Available on-site

FACILITIES: Rentals, lessons, minor repairs, bike wash, washrooms, vending machines.

ADMISSION: $4, season's pass $60.

REPAIR SHOP: Missing Link, 1283 Commissioners Road W., 519-641-5056. All Seasons Sport and Cycle, 790 Dundas Street, 519-660-6932. Cyclepath, 737 Richmond Street, 519-432-2208. Racer Sportif, 353 Clarence Street, 519-434-5652.

TOURISM INFORMATION: Tourism London, 800-265-2602 or 519-661-5000, fax 519-661-6160, e-mail webmaster@city.london.on.ca www.city.london.on.ca

LAND MANGER: Boler Mountain Bike Centre, 519-657-8822, fax 519-657-8295, e-mail lsc@bolermountain.com www.bolermountain.com

Short Hills Provincial Park

◆ ◆◆ SOUTH OF ST. CATHARINES

Ratings

LENGTH: 10.5 km (6.5 miles)

TRAIL: Singletrack

SURFACE: Rugged hardpack with muddy patches

TECHNICAL: Hard to extreme

LAYOUT: Two mapped and blazed loops

TOPOGRAPHY: Hilly forest on the Niagara Escarpment

AESTHETICS: Waterfalls, ridges, valleys, and wildlife

IMPRESSION: Rambunctious, hardcore riding

Set on the Niagara Escarpment around the headwaters of Twelve Mile Creek and its many tributaries, Short Hills Provincial Park is a vast assembly of forested hills, open valleys, high ridges, fields and creeks. As one of a mere few legal riding areas in the St. Catharines and Niagara region, it's popular. Of the park's 60,000 seasonal visitors, 80 percent are fat-tire enthusiasts.

Officially, Short Hills has 10.5 km (6.5 miles) of trails available for mountain biking. Renegade offshoots, however, run rampant throughout this huge 735-ha (1,815 acre) property, and many of these informal trails are as wide and well worn as their formal counterparts. If you don't keep a constant eye out for yellow blazes, which mark the two official shared-use trails, you can easily get sidetracked.

Make every effort to stay on designated trails. As tempting as offshoots may be, they encroach wildlife habitats. Besides, the blazed way will keep you from getting lost for hours.

The two shared-use trails are the 6.2-km (4 mile) Swayze Falls and the 4.3-km (2.5 mile) Black Walnut. They are connected loops, each with a scenic waterfall. Gnarled old roots, deep mud patches, makeshift bridges, log obstacles at wonky angles, sharp ascents on loose rock and tight ridgelines with adjacent drop-offs, require vigilant riding.

You never know what lies ahead. Terrain is constantly changing and there's always mud somewhere, even after days of sunshine, due to the water-retaining clay base.

Getting hurt is easy on some rebel spurs. The unofficial trail descent that crosses the Black Walnut Trail has a big round rock in a wide grassy field in the park's center. It's too easy to fly perfectly in the air before crashing and being carried out in a stretcher.

Those who carefully negotiate their way will appreciate the hemlock groves, ancient trees, waterfalls in alcoves, and surrounding Carolinian Forest. This unusual southern flora includes sassafras, shagbark hickory, and black walnut.

Status

POLITICS: This environmentally sensitive park is over-used. Park management is trying to close a lot of the unofficial side trails to provide resting areas for the park's many animals. A volunteer community policing and patrolling program is in place in partnership with the OPP, Ontario Parks and Niagara College. Hikers and equestrians use the multi-use trails.

RESTRICTIONS: Stay off blue-blazed, hiking-only trails. Night riding is prohibited; riders caught after 10 P.M. are charged $65.

ETIQUETTE: Don't ride for at least two days after a rainfall; the clay base retains water and erodes easily. Stay on yellow-blazed trails.

CAUTIONS: Two-way traffic, blind corners, steep hills.

Short Hills Provincial Park

Short Hills Provincial Park

Guide Notes

NEAREST COMMUNITY: Thorold, Fonthill

LOCATION: Located 10 minutes from St. Catharines and 15 minutes from Niagara Falls, the park has three entrances with parking lots on Pelham Road, Wiley Road, and Rolland Road.

To reach the main entrance on Pelham Road, take the QEW (east of St. Catharines) to Highway 406 south to Beaverdam's Road. Go west to Merritville Highway, north to Decew Road, west to First Street, north to Pelham Road, west to Gilligan Road, south to the parking lot.

To reach the Roland Road. entrance — via St. John's Outdoor Study Centre — take Highway 406 south to Holland Road and go west. Holland Road turns into Roland Road at Cataract Road. St. John's Centre is about 0.6 km (0.4 miles) on your right-hand side. From here the park entrance is 1.7 km (1 mile).

TRAIL MAP: A trail guide book by Friends of Short Hills Park is available for $5 from St. John's Outdoor Study Centre and local outdoor stores.

FACILITIES: Three separate parking lots.

ADMISSION: Free

REPAIR SHOP: Thornton's Cycle and Sports, 300 Lincoln Street, Welland, 905-732-4770. Liberty Cycle, 40 St. Paul Street, St. Catharines, 905-682-1454.

TOURISM INFORMATION: Niagara Tourism, 800-263-2988 or 905-984-3626, fax 905-688-5907, e-mail destniag@tourismniagara.com www.tourismniagara.com

LAND MANAGER: Short Hills Provincial Park, 905-774-6642 www.ontparks.com

Ontario

Camp Fortune

Northumberland Forest

■ ■ ■ ■ NORTH OF COBOURG

Ratings

LENGTH: 40 km (25 miles)

TRAIL: Singletrack and doubletrack

SURFACE: Hardpacked sandy topsoil

TECHNICAL: Easy to moderate

LAYOUT: Mapped and marked network of one-way loops

TOPOGRAPHY: Bright leafy forest, deer sightings

IMPRESSION: Big-ring singletrack speedway

Mountain bikers have cross-country skiers to thank for the great network of well-marked, mapped and color-coded loops that snake through the hills of Northumberland Forest.

The green trail, the longest of four loops, is best. A twisty singletrack, it swoops over hills and along the tops of ridges where wooden benches invite a rest. A 15-km (9 mile) romp leads through bright hardwood forest and spacious pine plantation. Treetops are tall, trunks are spread out, saplings and blackberry bushes strive in the undergrowth.

Pace your energy for the hills, especially the Hogsback, a.k.a. Johnny Puke — a grunting, knee-buster climb — and beware of intermittent sand patches. Sandy topsoil throughout provides excellent drainage, but creates beach-like segments during dry spells. Moreover, trails in this soft soil have been worn into shallow trenches with berms on every turn. Downhills can be skied with mean leans in corners.

The way is smooth, with the exception of ancient rock-pile property lines. Hybrid bikes fare fine and numerous sections grant fast big-ring riding. Families tentative about singletrack can alternatively enjoy the intertwining crisscross of fireroads. These doubletrack trails also allow riders to shortcut or lengthen routes.

The trail network weaves through only a small portion of Northumberland's huge 2,640-ha (6,600 acre) forest, but riders may nevertheless not see another soul en route — even when the parking lot is full.

Status

POLITICS: Northumberland Forest is a multi-use recreational area, owned and managed by Northumberland County with trails maintained by various trail-user groups. Hikers, equestrians, dirt bikes, ATVs, hunters and cross-country skiers also use trails.

ETIQUETTE: Respect adjacent private property.

MAINTENANCE: Mountain bikers organize maintenance days in spring and fall; contact Proform Cycle and Accessories, 905-885-4857.

CAUTIONS: Poison ivy is common throughout the forest and is particularly prominent on the red trail. Hunters frequent the forest during hunting season in spring and fall.

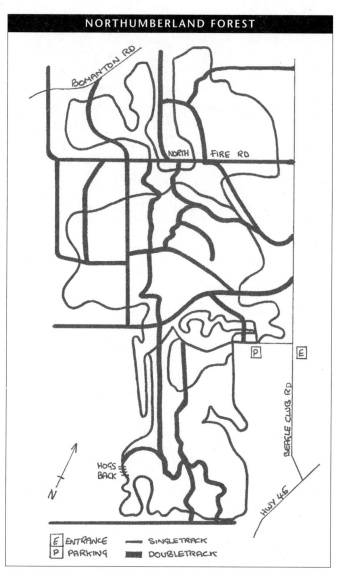

Northumberland Forest

Guide Notes

NEAREST COMMUNITY: Cobourg

LOCATION: From Highway 401, take Highway 45 north 14 km (8.5 miles) to Beagle Club Road, turn left and go 1 km (0.6 miles) to the parking lot on your left.

TRAIL MAP: Maps are posted throughout the forest and are available from Northumberland Tourism.

FACILITIES: Parking lot

ADMISSION: Free

TIPS: Hybrid bikes are suitable. Conditions are best after a rainfall. The northeast section is rough, overgrown, extremely sandy, and barely rideable.

REPAIR SHOP: Proform Cycle and Accessories, on Highway 2 between Port Hope and Cobourg, 905-885-4857.

TOURISM INFORMATION: Northumberland Tourism, 905-372-0141 or 800-354-7050, e-mail tourism@eagle.ca www.eagle.ca/tourism/

LAND MANAGER: Northumberland County, 905-372-0141 or 800-354-7050.

GROUP RIDES: Wednesday night with Proform Cycle and Accessories, 905-885-4857.

Goodrich-Loomis Conservation Area ㉗

Ratings

LENGTH: 14 km (9 miles)

TRAIL: Wide track

SURFACE: Hardpack, grass swaths, roots, and muddy sections

TECHNICAL: Easy to hard

LAYOUT: Network of six trails

TOPOGRAPHY: High-rolling hills with a creek, wetland, mixed forest, oak savannah, and prairie remnants

AESTHETICS: Panoramic view, cedar groves, streamside trails, bridge crossings, and bluebirds

IMPRESSION: Challenging variations

Goodrich-Loomis Conservation Area is an extremely diverse park that encompasses two high ridges on either side of Cold Creek. Trails run alongside the creek, on top of the northern ridge, down into lowland cedar groves, over bridges, and through mature mixed forest.

The six marked and mapped trails present different pockets of this hilly, 350-ha (865 acre) park. Terrain and technical difficulty varies considerably, though trails are wide and great for group rides.

Take the Esker Trail for a long ascent through a swath of grass to a breezy ridge for a view over Northumberland Hills. Barrel down to the Loop D'Loop and face a snotty alcove of roots, axle-deep mud pits, corduroy log patches, and fallen trees that require bike hoisting. Avoid the Beaver Trail, which is worse, and peel alongside the shaded creek to the bridge crossing into the bright and dry Pine Loop.

Expect some brutal climbs and also many hiker encounters. Former fast, blind turns have been clear-cut for safety. The park has a provincially significant wetland, an established bluebird population, and many rare plant species. Numerous interpretation stations can be found en route.

Status

POLITICS: The Lower Trent Mountain Bike Association patrols the park. It is heavily used by hikers.

CAUTIONS: Two-way traffic, poison ivy in spots, mosquitoes bad in spring and summer.

Guide Notes

NEAREST COMMUNITY: Brighton

LOCATION: From Highway 401, go north 6.4 km (4 miles) on Highway 30, turn left on Goodrich Road and follow conservation signs approx. 5 km (3 mile). Entrance is on your left-hand side.

TRAIL MAP: Available on-site.

FACILITIES: Outhouses

ADMISSION: Free

REPAIR SHOP: A Motion Industries, 204 Dundas E., Trenton, 613-962-1809.

TOURISM INFORMATION: Trenton and District Chamber of Commerce, 800-930-3255 or 613-392-7635, fax 613-394-8400.

LAND MANAGER: Lower Trent Conservation Authority, 613-394-4829, fax 613-394-5226

GROUP RIDES: Lower Trent Mountain Bike Association runs group rides on the last Sunday of every month during summer and fall; for details check with the Land Manager. A Motion Industries offers Wednesday night and Sunday fun rides, 613-962-1809.

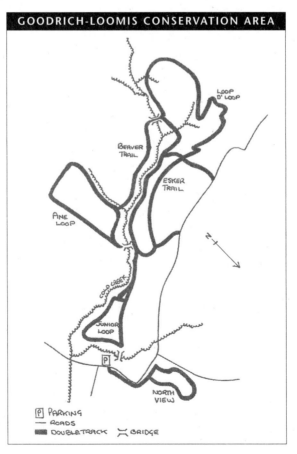

GOODRICH-LOOMIS CONSERVATION AREA

Macaulay Mountain Conservation Area

 PICTON

Ratings

LENGTH: 20 km (12.5 miles)

TRAIL: Singletrack

SURFACE: Hardpack with soft, rooty sections

TECHNICAL: Hard to extreme

LAYOUT: Unmarked, unmapped network on the bottom, top and slope of an escarpment

TOPOGRAPHY: 40-meter (131 foot) forested escarpment

AESTHETICS: Lookout platforms, hemlock stands, varied terrain, a field of 80 different birdhouses

IMPRESSION: Engaging creation

When the Bloomfield Bicycle Club began reclaiming old trails at Macaulay Mountain Conservation Area in 1996, the club members and other local riding enthusiasts gathered religiously on-site, Tuesday nights, to create a highly stimulating singletrack playground.

The conservation area encompasses a 40-meter (131 foot) escarpment in the shape of a question mark. Its slopes are covered in mixed forest, hemlock stands, and cedar groves with the exception of a few cleared streaks in the east where tubing and tobogganing are offered in winter. Threading the park are 11 km (7 miles) of hiking and cross-country skiing trails. Three main routes stretch the length of the escarpment: along the bottom, the top and middle.

Essentially, Bloomfield Bicycle Club developed up and down transitions between main trails, along with a tightly wound ball of track through hemlock in the bowl of the escarpment's question mark. Bridges were built, traverses were reinforced, and a windchime of bicycle tubes was hung along a series of hairpin turns they call Groovy Tuesday.

While the main trails, which have been around for years, are singletrack challenges in their own right, with roots, rocks and serious climbs, the new trails are nervy. Transitions are steep and deep with gnarly narrow traverses. The maze of track in the hemlock bowl twists over a rattle of roots with quick drops and climbs among handlebar-width tree trunks. Get to the top and you're on a flat, gravel-strewn ridge run through maples to platforms overlooking Picton Bay.

Status

POLITICS: Trails are open to all non-motorized users during daylight hours. Hikers frequent them. More beginners and intermediate trails are planned for development, as well as trailhead maps and trail signposts.

EVENTS: Cornstock Survivors Ride, Labour Day; contact Bloomfield.

MAINTENANCE: Regular trail maintenance days; contact Bloomfield.

CAUTIONS: Be extra cautious in wet conditions on roots and bridges.

Macaulay Mountain Conservation Area

Guide Notes

NEAREST COMMUNITY: Picton, Bloomfield, Belleville

LOCATION: From Highway 401, go south on Highway 62 to Bloomfield then east on Highway 33 into Picton. At the east end of town, turn right on Union Street and go 1 km. Park entrance is on your right.

TRAIL MAP: Hiking maps available on-site; they do not include new trails.

FACILITIES: Parking, picnic tables beside a pond. Nearby camping is available at numerous parks including Sandbanks Provincial Park. Also, a wide variety of hotels, motels, inns and B&Bs are in the area.

ADMISSION: Free

TIPS: For the most fun, ask the bike shop for a local guide to show you the trails.

REPAIR SHOP: Bloomfield Bicycle Co., 225 Main Street, Bloomfield, 613-393-1060, e-mail bbc@reach.net Doug's Bicycles, Belleville, 159 College W., and 613-966-9161.

TOURISM INFORMATION: Prince Edward County Tourism, 800-640-4717, fax 613-476-7461, e-mail pec@connect.reach.net www.pec.on.ca

LAND MANAGER: Prince Edward Regional Conservation Authority, 613-476-7408.

GROUP RIDES: Sunday club rides, including Chick Rides, and monthly community rides, with Bloomfield Bicycle Club (see Repair Shop).

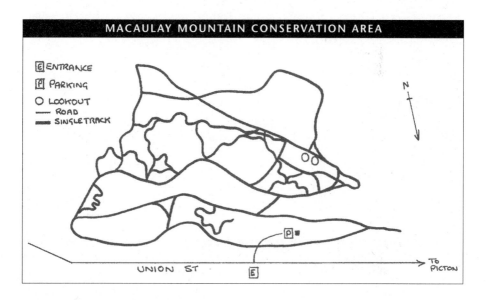

MACAULAY MOUNTAIN CONSERVATION AREA

Silent Lake Provincial Park

| | | | SOUTH OF BANCROFT |

Ratings

LENGTH: 21 km (13 miles)

TRAIL: Singletrack

SURFACE: Hardpack with mud patches, roots, rocks

TECHNICAL: Moderate to hard

LAYOUT: 13 km (8 miles) out-and-back, 19-km (12 mile) loop, mapped and well-marked

TOPOGRAPHY: Relatively flat forest in the Kawartha Highlands

AESTHETICS: Wilderness setting, cool boardwalk, wildflowers, mixed forest, bogs, marshes

IMPRESSION: A long quiet interlude, not for families

Silent Lake Provincial Park challenges intermediate-level mountain bikers with a 19-km (12 mile) singletrack loop with no way out but forward or back. Once you pass the 6-km mark, you're committed. A sign warns: "Be aware, the remaining trail is difficult and challenging. It will take you two hours to reach the parking area." Believe the sign and plan for even longer.

Newly opened to mountain biking in 1998, this cross-country ski trail has a 4-km (2.5 mile) stretch that's raw with sucking soft soil, mossy rock gardens and decomposing, slippery corduroy logs. Until this section is packed down and broken in by enduring use, it warrants sweat, tears and words your mother wouldn't want to hear. But reach the shelter cabin at the 12-km mark and you've reached easy street, comparatively. From here, the trail is hardpacked with roots, rocks and mere mud pockets.

Less aggressive bikers can opt for an out-and-back, 13-km (8 mile) trip to the "Be aware..." sign. The way is wide and hardpacked, though moderately technical. Do ride, however, to the boardwalk — just 2 km (1.2 miles) past the sign. The raw section lies beyond it, and the boardwalk is a pretty spot at an intersection of hiking, biking and canoeing routes. Moreover, the 240-meter-long (800 foot) structure, built with turns and banks over a stream and swamp linking Silent Lake to Quiet Lake, drums a cool beat under your tires.

Whatever your choice, you'll be immersed in a relatively flat forest filled with maple, birch, hemlock and white pine, passing lakes, ponds and marshes.

Silent Lake Provincial Park

Status

POLITICS: Silent Lake is one of a handful of provincial parks allowing mountain biking.

RESTRICTIONS: Stay off hiking trails.

ETIQUETTE: Helmets mandatory. Overnight camping along the trail or in trail shelters is not permitted.

MAINTENANCE: Bancroft Broken Spokes Mountain Bike Club organizes maintenance days, 613-332-1969.

CAUTIONS: The trail crosses the park access road at two locations near the beginning; be mindful of cars. Also, there's two-way bike traffic on the first 4 km (2.5 miles).

Guide Notes

NEAREST COMMUNITY: Bancroft

LOCATION: Located on Highway 28, 24 km (15 miles) north of Apsley and 25 km (15.5 miles) south of Bancroft.

TRAIL MAP: Available at the park office.

FACILITIES: Camping, rental yurts, rental lodge for groups, separate hiking trails, canoe and kayak rentals, swimming, fishing, interpretive programs.

ADMISSION: $7.50 per vehicle. Open for biking mid-May to mid-October.

TIPS: Best conditions are July to October; stay away during bug-infested spring.

REPAIR SHOP: The Bike Shop, 10 Hastings Street N., Bancroft; has rentals, 613-332-1969.

TOURISM INFORMATION: Bancroft & District Chamber of Commerce, 613-332-1513, fax 613-332-2119, e-mail chamber@commerce.bancroft.on.ca www.commerce.bancroft.on.ca

LAND MANAGER: Silent Lake Provincial Park, 613-339-2807 (Park Office) or 613-332-3940, www.ontparks.com

CLUBS/TOURS: Clubs: see Maintenance. Tours: Trips and Trails takes groups on 1- to 3-day-long singletrack excursions on Crown land and private land where land access permission has been obtained. Bike and canoe combination trips also offered. 800-481-2925 or 613-332-1969 www.mwdesign.net/tipstail.html

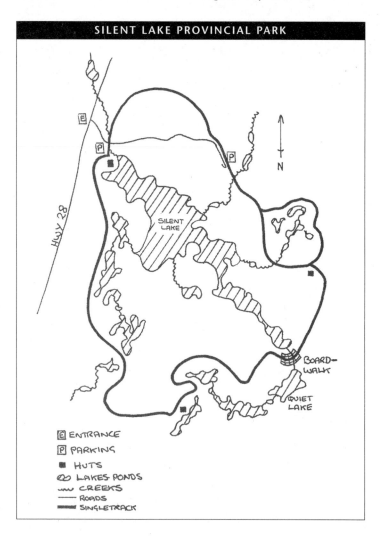

Kanata Lakes

KANATA, WEST OF OTTAWA

Ratings

LENGTH: 20 km (12 miles)

TRAIL: Singletrack and a wide gravel pathway

SURFACE: Hardpack with roots and Canadian Shield rock

TECHNICAL: Hard singletrack, easy pathway

LAYOUT: Mostly mapped but unmarked trail network

TOPOGRAPHY: Canadian Shield rock and forest

AESTHETICS: Rock slabs, marshes, old trees

IMPRESSION: Rocky playhouse

The subdivision of Kanata Lakes has a funky network of forested singletrack trails. At least for now. The land is owned by developers who have major subdivision plans by the year 2015. Until construction begins, the land is available for multi-recreational use, thanks to negotiations by the City of Kanata.

Straddling both sides of Goulbourn Forest Road, trails weave among trees, skirt marshes and roll over slabs of Canadian Shield rock. The land is relatively flat, but rock outcrops present steep climbs and dives. As well, there are tricky rooty sections, mud patches and corduroy log bridges.

The west side is more technical than the east side, and is site to a race series organized by Kunstadt Sports. Main routes here have been signed by cross-country ski clubs, while offshoots, created by mountain bikers, are unmarked. All trails, however, loop faithfully back to the access road.

East side trails lead to a manmade pond and connect to a wide, gravel pathway, ideal for family riding.

Status

POLITICS: Trails are frequented by hikers.

EVENTS: Race series, organized by Kunstadt Sports, 613-432-1234.

CAUTIONS: Don't bike beyond the hydro corridor in the west; be careful at road and railway crossings.

Kanata Lakes

Guide Notes

NEAREST TOWN/CITY: Kanata

LOCATION: From Ottawa on Highway 417 (The Queensway), exit Eagleson Road and go west 3 km (2 miles) on Campeau Drive, turn right on Castlefrank Road — which turns into Richardson Side Road — and go north 2 km (1.2 miles), turn right onto Goulbourn Forest Rd and go 1 km (0.6 miles) to the parking lot on your right-hand side. Trails are on both sides of the road. If approaching from the east on Highway 417, exit at Terry Fox Road and go north, turn right on Campeau Drive, then left at Castlefrank Road and continue with directions noted above.

TRAIL MAP/INFO: Cross-country ski maps are posted at the parking lot and are available from Kanata Parks and Recreation, 613-592-4291, fax 613-592-8183.

FACILITIES: Parking lot

ADMISSION: Free

REPAIR SHOP: Kunstadt Sports, 462 Hazeldean Rd, Kanata, 613-831-2059.

TOURISM INFO: Ottawa Tourism, 800-363-4465 or 613-237-6822, fax 613-237-7339 www.tourottawa.org

LAND MANAGER: Owned by Genstar Development Corporation with an agreement with the City of Kanata.

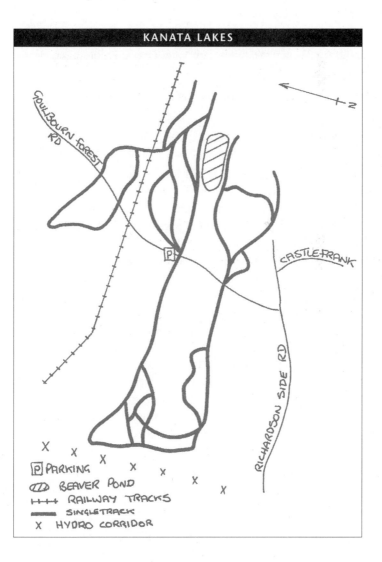

Camp Fortune

31

◆◆◆ GATINEAU PARK, HULL, NORTH OF OTTAWA

Ratings

LENGTH: 14 km (9 miles)

TRAIL: Singletrack and doubletrack

SURFACE: Rooty, muddy hardpack with loose rocks

TECHNICAL: Hard to extreme

LAYOUT: 5- and 9-km (3 and 5.5 mile) race loops, marked on a ski hill

TOPOGRAPHY: 183-meter (620 foot) hill with hardwood forest and cleared slopes

AESTHETICS: View of the Gatineau Hills

IMPRESSION: Gritty, muddy, demanding and intimidating

On the Quebec Cup Circuit and host to the 1998 Quebec Championships, Camp Fortune is a serious destination with one of the toughest race courses in eastern Canada. An alpine ski resort in winter, it transforms into an elitist fat-tire stage in off-season.

Spectators line the slopes on Wednesdays to witness the downhill and cross-country events, held alternatively each week. The grueling cross-country race, with 5- and 9-km (3 and 5.5 mile) loops, attracts up to 200 riders.

Located in Gatineau Park, Camp Fortune is a rough and radical alternative to the park's otherwise sedentary trail network. Top racers had a field day designing courses on this 183-meter (620 foot) hill with two summits, cleared slopes, forest patches and ski access roads.

The two marked cross-country loops begin at the hill base on a rocky, muddy, pot-holed doubletrack. The climb is brutal, not just in length, but in severity of pitch. Reach the top and the real test begins. Routes oscillate in the upper reaches with precipitous pitches, acute turns, slippery switchbacks and relentless undulations. Forested terrain is uneven, slopes are strewn with loose rocks, and permanent mudholes are so deep they'll grease your knees.

Seventy percent of the trails are singletrack with roots, rocks and log obstacles. Overall, the Valley side, above the chalet, is more forgiving than the Skyline side with its drop-offs and other sardonic amusements.

Status

EVENTS: Wednesday night race series with alternating downhill and cross-country events. Kids camp, women's camps, and lessons, offered by Creative Wheel, 613-860-0887. Chairlifts run mid-September to mid-October, during which period Sunday brunches are available.

Camp Fortune

Guide Notes

NEAREST COMMUNITY: Ottawa, Hull

LOCATION: 15 minutes north from Ottawa. From Highway 417, exit at Nicholas and follow signs to Hull/King Edward Street N, go across the MacDonald/Cartier Bridge and follow Highway 5 about 10 km (6 miles) to Old Chelsea (Exit 12). Turn left at the stop sign and follow Old Chelsea/Meech Road for 4 km (2.5 miles) to the Camp Fortune access road, turn left.

TRAIL MAP: Not available

FACILITIES: Washrooms, bike wash on-site. Elsewhere in Gatineau Park, camping, shared-use trails, hiking-only trails, more (see Gatineau Park).

ADMISSION: Free

TIPS: For transportation from Ottawa, plus nearby youth hostel accommodation, see Tips in Gatineau Park.

REPAIR SHOP: Greg Christie's Ski & Cycle Works, 148 Old Chelsea Road, 819-827-5340. Gerry & Isobels, 14 Scott Road, Old Chelsea, 819-827-4341.

TOURISM INFORMATION: Ottawa Tourism, 613-237-6822 or 800-363-4465, fax 613-237-7339 www.tourottawa.org

LAND MANAGER: Camp Fortune, 819-827-1717 or 888-283-1717, fax 819-827-3893, e-mail Information@campfortune.com www.campfortune.com

GROUP RIDES: Tuesday and Wednesday nights to various areas with Tommy & Lefebvre, 613-236-9731.

Gatineau Park

32

██ ██ ▌ HULL, NORTH OF OTTAWA

Ratings

LENGTH: 90 km (56 miles)

TRAIL: Wide singletrack and doubletrack

SURFACE: Gravel, rooty hardpack, fireroads

TECHNICAL: Easy to moderate

LAYOUT: 19 trails with links for loops and extensions

TOPOGRAPHY: Forested lofty hills, lakes, meadows

AESTHETICS: Camping, historic sites, lookouts

IMPRESSION: Holiday biking with camping options

Gatineau Park has all the ingredients for a mountain biking vacation. It has long trails, camping areas, and destinations, including historic sites, beaches, caves and lookouts. Its 35,200-ha (88,000 acre) domain is a mosaic of hills and lakes, mature forests, wildflower-strewn meadows and granite cliffs.

Pack your tent and sleeping bag and link Trails 36 and 50 for a 20-km (12.5 mile), one-way trip to the Lac Philippe camping area. Starting at the O'Brien parking lot — you can swim nearby in a lake from a beach — the trail is hard-packed with roots, rocks, and stream crossings on narrow wooden bridges. Stop for lunch at the shelter of Herridge Lodge, an 1880s farm house. Before reaching the camping area, take a short hike to Lusk Caves and follow a stream through skylit caverns.

There are 19 different shared-use trails covering 90 km (56 miles) of winding track. They are mapped, well marked, well maintained, color-coded and numbered. Accessible from various parking lots, most trails connect with others, allowing for loops, extensions and links to towns.

Prefer a bed to a sleeping bag? Consider lodging at a bed and breakfast in the quaint villages of Old Chelsea, near the park's south end, or Wakefield, near the north end. Both villages have direct access to park trails.

Most trails are wide corridors and all have extensive hills, some steep, others gradual and seemingly endless. Trail 1 rises 100 meters (328 feet) in less than 500 meters (1,640 feet). Trail 52 has a continuous climb for 6 km (3.7 miles) — but ride north toward Wakefield and that climb translates into one serious downhill.

Surfaces vary considerably, from the fireroads of Trail 50, to the soft gravel on Trail 1 — a 20-km (12.5 mile) route that leads up to a firetower — to the hardpack on Trails 5 and 15 that together bring you to the estate grounds of the former Prime Minister Mackenzie King.

Status

POLITICS: The park has a lot of great singletrack trails that are unfortunately off-limits to mountain bikers due to their environmental sensitivity. Volunteer bike rangers patrol on weekends from mid-August through fall.

RESTRICTIONS: Green-color-coded trails are for hikers only.

ETIQUETTE: Respect trail closures and the rules of the park.

Guide Notes

NEAREST COMMUNITY: Hull, Ottawa

LOCATION: 15 minutes from Ottawa. From Highway 417, exit at Nicholas and follow signs to Hull/King Edward Street N., go across the MacDonald/Cartier Bridge and follow Highway 5 10 km (6 miles) to Old Chelsea (Exit 12). Turn left at the stop sign and follow Old Chelsea/Meech Road for 2 km (1.2 miles) to the Visitor's Centre on your right-hand side.

TRAIL MAP/INFORMATION: Maps $3, available at Gatineau Park Visitor Centre, 819-827-2020, e-mail gpvisito@ncc-ccn.ca

FACILITIES: Camping at Lac Philippe and Lac Taylor. The Brown Lake Cabin, equipped with cooking facilities, pots and utensils, is available for rent. Eight day-use shelters with wood stoves and safety radio systems are scattered throughout the park.

ADMISSION: Open mid-May to the end of November, with $6 per car access fees in effect June to September in the Lac Philippe, Meech Lake and Mackenzie King Estate sectors.

TIPS: For a wholesome meal, go to Gerry & Isobel's in Old Chelsea near the park's southeastern boundary. An old-fashioned steam train — with special racks for bikes — runs from Hull to Wakefield, May to the end of October, 800-871-7246 or 819-778-7246. Back Country Bus Adventures offers pickup from major hotels and bus and train stations in Ottawa to various trailheads in the park, including the one at the Carman Trails Youth Hostel (819-459-3180 www.magma.ca/~carman) near Wakefield, and to Camp Fortune; return cost ranges from $15 to $22, 613-851-7045 or 819-459-3180 www.magma.ca/~bcb.html.

REPAIR SHOP: Greg Christie's Ski & Cycle Works, 148 Old Chelsea Rd, 819-827-5340. Gerry & Isobel's, 14 Scott Road, Old Chelsea, 819-827-4341.

TOURISM INFORMATION: Ottawa Tourism, 800-363-4465 or 613-237-6822, fax 613-237-7339 www.tourottawa.org

LAND MANAGER: National Capital Commission, 800-465-1867, fax 819-827-3337 www.capcan.ca

GROUP RIDES: Tuesday and Wednesday nights to various sites with Tommy & Lefebvre, 613-236-9731.

Ontario

Grandview Inn Nature Trails

Porcupine Ridge (33)

 ◆ ◆◆ SANTA'S VILLAGE, BRACEBRIDGE

Ratings

LENGTH: 25 km (15.5 miles)

TRAIL: Singletrack

SURFACE: Hardpack with roots, rocks, mud

TECHNICAL: Hard to extreme

LAYOUT: One main loop with 17 offshoots, all marked, mapped, rated

TOPOGRAPHY: Canadian Shield rock, mixed forest, three major ridges, and two creeks

AESTHETICS: View of Lake Muskoka, cliffs, variety of terrain

IMPRESSION: Advanced, concentrated technical theme park

To know fear or have no fear? That is the question at Porcupine Ridge, a gutsy park with relentless challenge. What doesn't make you freeze, walk or turn back will make you stronger, more aggressive and determined. If you're not unnerved, you'll be pushing your limits.

Trails are warped and turbulent. They hinge around trees and throb through rocks. They have root-entangled climbs and sheer granite drops. Turns are tight and continual. Dares are constant. When you're not cranking up a steep protuberance, you're hanging your backside behind in a dive. When you're not hoisting your front end over a log, you're twisting among trunks on gnarly slopes. Always negotiating, gripping hard, sweating volumes while pedaling at a crawl.

Trails were designed with B.C.'s North Shore in mind. Inspired by a visit to North America's most radical and defying trail system, Ian Dawes, owner of Ecclestone Cycle, spun a deal with Santa's Village. On their 48-ha (120 acre) property, he would design, build and maintain a trail park in return for a life-time admission of riding. Beginning in the winter of 1997, Dawes and friends donned snowshoes and flagged animal tracks. In spring they cut and clipped routes — thanking the trees before they fell.

One main loop has 17 different offshoots that branch away at intervals. The 3.5-km (2 mile) main loop is a semi-technical, wide singletrack that leads to a ridge overlooking Lake Muskoka. You'll need a breather between the storm of offshoots as you work your way around, picking and choosing among options. Marked and rated, the offshoots are short — merely a kilometer (less than a mile) in length on average — though some are linked with others, offering extensions.

Moreover, "secret" spurs, not marked on the map, are marked along the way with squat purple gremlins. Follow at your own risk; these spurs lead to radical sites where groupies spend hours riding a plank on a cliff, hopping blocks of rock, or peeling down a rotund boulder with a compression base.

Status

POLITICS: Porcupine Ridge Singletrack Centre is located on the property of Santa's Village, a family theme park.

EVENTS: Tuesday night race series, organized by Ecclestone (see Repair Shop).

CAUTIONS: Mosquitoes throughout the season.

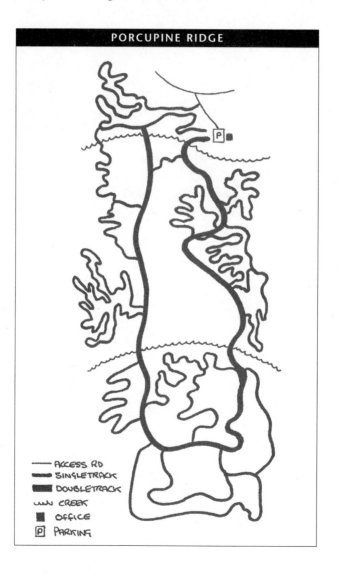

PORCUPINE RIDGE

ACCESS RD
SINGLETRACK
DOUBLETRACK
CREEK
OFFICE
PARKING

Porcupine Ridge

Guide Notes

NEAREST COMMUNITY: Bracebridge

LOCATION: From Highway 11, take Highway 118 west to Bracebridge, go through the first set of traffic lights and turn left at Santa's Village Road. Continue 5 km. Porcupine Ridge is on the right-hand side next to Santa's Village.

TRAIL MAP: Detailed maps available at the Centre.

FACILITIES: Parking, rentals, camping (705-645-5682), family theme park with rides, go-carts, mini-golf, inline skating and more.

ADMISSION: $5 trail pass

REPAIR SHOP: Ecclestone Cycle Co., also has rentals, 230 Ecclestone Drive, Bracebridge, 705-645-1166, e-mail bicycle@muskoka.com www.muskoka.com/bicycle

TOURISM INFORMATION: Muskoka Tourism, 800-267-9700 or 705-689-0660, fax 705-689-9118, e-mail Information@muskoka-tourism.on.ca www.muskoka-tourism.on.ca

LAND MANAGER: Santa's Village, 705-645-2512.

GROUP RIDES: Wednesday nights and Sunday mornings to various areas in Muskoka with Ecclestone Cycle.

Bracebridge Resource Management Centre

⬤ ◼ ▦ ▦   NORTH OF BRACEBRIDGE

Ratings

LENGTH: 9.5 km (6 miles)

TRAIL: Doubletrack and singletrack

SURFACE: Hardpack and freshly bulldozed stretches

TECHNICAL: Easy to moderate

LAYOUT: 5 interconnected loops

TOPOGRAPHY: Lightly rolling terrain, hardwood forest, pine plantation

AESTHETICS: Riverside and cliff-base trails, pine-needle-covered corridors, forest information signs

IMPRESSION: Shaded carpet ride, fine for kids, with rugged, rutted options

Bracebridge Resource Management Area offers easy-rolling, slow-winding, pretty paths that are mapped and marked. It has a doubletracked main loop with four wide singletrack trails arranged around it like flower petals.

The way is smooth and hardpacked with no tight corners, steep climbs or technical obstacles. You're led through a mature pine plantation on a soft mat of needles and among mixed forest and hemlock groves. You'll cross bridges, pass erratic boulders, pedal beside the Muskoka River and along the base of a cliff. Signs describe land features and tree types, their needs and harvest time.

Riders will also find unmapped, unmarked secondary trails with greater challenge in the southwest end. Beware. One leads to a bulldozed passageway that's a muddy, tire-sucking swath with regurgitated earth and flailing root tentacles. Fresh cut passageways dampen and temper in time, but such trail "shaping" practices can be expected in this forest.

Status

POLITICS: The Bracebridge Resource Management Centre is Crown land. Trails are multi-use, frequented by hikers and equestrians, and used for cross-country skiing in winter.

Bracebridge Resource Management Centre

Guide Notes

NEAREST COMMUNITY: Bracebridge

LOCATION: On Highway 11 north of Bracebridge, on the east side, 2.5 km (1.5 miles) north of Highway 117.

TRAIL MAP: Posted at the parking lot and at trail intersections.

FACILITIES: Parking lot

ADMISSION: Free

REPAIR SHOP: Ecclestone Cycle Co., 230 Ecclestone Drive, Bracebridge, 705-645-1166.

TOURISM INFORMATION: Muskoka Tourism, 800-267-9700 or 705-689-0660, fax 705-689-9118, e-mail Information@muskoka-tourism.on.ca www.muskoka-tourism.on.ca

LAND TENURE: Managed by the Ministry of Natural Resources (Bracebridge Area Office, RR 2, Bracebridge, P1L 1W9), the town of Bracebridge and local clubs.

GROUP RIDES: Wednesday nights and Sunday morning group rides to various areas in Muskoka with Ecclestone Cycle Co, 705-645-1166, e-mail bicycle@muskoka.com www.muskoka.com/bicycle

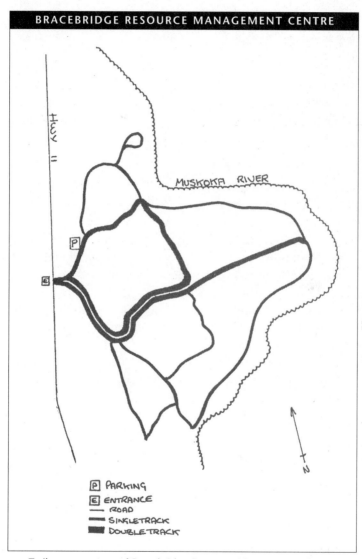

BRACEBRIDGE RESOURCE MANAGEMENT CENTRE

P PARKING
E ENTRANCE
— ROAD
— SINGLETRACK
— DOUBLETRACK

Trail map courtesy of Bracebridge Resource Management Centre

Moose Woods Trail Centre

 NORTHWEST OF HALIBURTON VILLAGE

Ratings

LENGTH: 35 km (22 miles)

TRAIL: Logging roads and singletrack

SURFACE: Gravel and hardpack

TECHNICAL: Easy to hard

LAYOUT: Mapped and well-marked network

TOPOGRAPHY: Hilly hardwood forest

AESTHETICS: Possible bear, moose and deer sightings

IMPRESSION: Invigorating, satisfying

Inspired by the outdoor enthusiasm of his nephew, landowner Wolf Fluegel transformed his logging forest into a recreational playground in the summer of 1996 and called it the Moose Woods Trail Centre. Today, with a total of 35 km (22 miles) of trails, the property offers three main doubletracked loops and more than half a dozen singletrack offshoots, all well-marked, signed and one-way.

The doubletrack trails are well-worn tracks that allow side-by-side riding on former logging roads. They present constant climbs with respective descents through rolling hardwood forest. One playful area is near the end of the Energizer Loop, where the trail breaks out of the greenery into a clearing of hydropower lines. Under the buzz of overhead wires, you're led over a succession of roly-poly mounds.

The newer singletrack trails are short, but technical, with steeps, roots and rocks. For a big bite of challenge, check out the Ridge at the property's far end.

Status

POLITICS: Trails are also used for hiking, horseback riding, cross-country skiing and snowshoeing.

EVENTS: Site to a few races each season.

Guide Notes

NEAREST COMMUNITY: Haliburton

LOCATION: From the village of Haliburton, take Highway 118 west 5 km (3 miles) to County Road 14 and go north 3 km (2 miles).

TRAIL MAP: Available on-site.

FACILITIES: Parking, rentals, snacks, and refreshments

ADMISSION: $5 adults, $4 students, and $12 families

TIPS: Wear bug repellent.

REPAIR SHOP: Glen Sharpley Sports, Highland Street, Haliburton, 705-457-3933.

TOURISM INFORMATION: Haliburton Highlands Chamber of Commerce, 800-461-7677 or 705-286-1760, fax 705-286-6016, e-mail hhcc@cybernet.on.ca www.cybernet.on.ca/~hhcc

LAND MANAGER: Moose Woods Trail Centre, 705-754-4976, fax 705-754-4958, www.auriga.on.ca/hal/moose.html

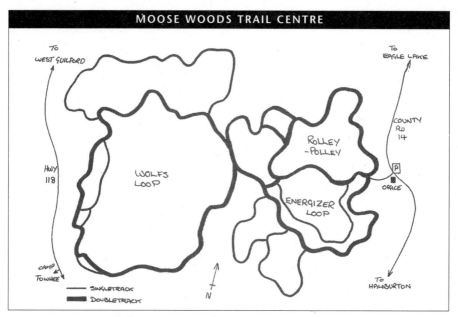

Trail map courtesy of Moose Woods Trail Centre

Haliburton Forest

■ ◆ ◆◆ NORTH OF HALIBURTON, SOUTH OF ALGONQUIN PARK

Ratings

LENGTH: 300 km (186 miles)

TRAIL: Singletrack and doubletrack

SURFACE: Hardpack with roots, rocks, mud holes

TECHNICAL: Easy to extreme

LAYOUT: Very well marked and mapped, rated network

TOPOGRAPHY: Forested hills of the Haliburton Highlands

AESTHETICS: Lookouts, marshes, wildlife sightings, mixed forest

IMPRESSION: Premier riding on a motherlode of trails

Check your ego at the gate and prepare to be humbled. Haliburton Forest, Ontario's most extensive mountain bike playground, is also the province's most intense.

On difficult and extreme-rated trails you'll face long, steep, corkscrew descents, seemingly endless climbs, gnarly narrow traverses, root canals, rock gullies, stream crossings, mud holes, and a sense of boundlessness. Sweat will pour, adrenaline will surge, and hearts will pound. Every stretch will reap accomplishment. And as you conquer, you'll feel invincible. And just as you begin to laugh at the world, you'll be tossed like a peanut, clear over your handlebars.

The trails of Haliburton Forest can easily punish cockiness. Tough trails are unyielding. All trails — even those rated as moderate and easy — devour twice as much time as expected. They run high and low through a vast 20,000-ha (50,000 acre) wilderness encompassing massive hills and more than 50 lakes. The sheer volume of its 300-km (186 mile) network could constitute a week-long, fat-tire mega-marathon.

Trails form loops, unraveling the shores of lakes, busting straight up hills through thick stands of fir, running ridges studded with maple and birch, then down, coursing rocky ravines. They streak through enormous fields of raspberries, past marshes spiked with bulrushes, over bare rock outcrops and up twisty, rooted slopes. Where they don't loop, they dead-end with a picnic table at a pretty shore or lookout summit.

A snowmobiling domain in winter, Haliburton Forest — a privately owned property — opened its sledding tracks to mountain bikes in 1992, and since has cut more than a dozen additional mountain-bike-specific singletrack trails. All are clearly marked, mapped and rated; though some are better worn and smooth than others. The quality of riding, however, is exceptional throughout.

The probability of seeing wildlife — a moose, bear, deer, bobcat, otter, beaver, porcupine or wolf — is high. Six shelter cabins are on the trail system along with a handful of semi-wilderness lakeside campsites.

Gravel roads, which offer non-technical, beautiful meanders, lead to the mass array of trailheads. From base camp you can ride the roads to the trailheads, or drive — up to an hour away — to further reaches.

Status

POLITICS: Haliburton Forest and Wildlife Reserve is a privately owned, multi-use property.

ETIQUETTE: Respect the privacy of campsites; don't cross trailer or tent sites when going for a swim.

EVENTS: Mountain Bike Festival, a weekend event held annually in September.

CAUTIONS: Biting insects are brutal in spring and summer. Carry tools, first-aid equipment, food and lots of water. As a precaution, bring a compass.

Guide Notes

NEAREST COMMUNITY: Haliburton

LOCATION: South of Algonquin Provincial Park, take Highway 400 north to Barrie, Highway 11 north to Muskoka Falls, Highway 118 west to West Guilford, and Kennisis Lake Road (County Road 7) north to its end and follow signs.

TRAIL MAP: Available at the Gatehouse.

FACILITIES: Housekeeping units, dormitory-style beds, semi-wilderness lakeside campsites, a restaurant, store, mountain bike rentals, three interpretive walking trails, a logging museum. Forest Canopy Tours feature a boardwalk through treetops. The Wolf Centre, a research and education facility, houses a pack of gray wolves in a 6-ha (15 acre) enclosure.

ADMISSION: $10, camping $10; lodging ranges from $19 to $29. Open daily from mid-May to mid-October.

TIPS: If you don't have a good bike, rent one. Bring a waistbag to carry the trail map — you'll need it. Before heading out, ask staff for recommendations; some difficult-rated trails are more difficult than others; some moderate-rated trails are easier than others. Be sure to visit the intriguing Wolf Centre.

REPAIR SHOP: Glen Sharpley Sports, Highland Street, Haliburton, 705-457-3933.

Tourism Information: Haliburton Highlands Chamber of Commerce, 800-461-7677 or 705-286-1760, fax 705-286-6016, e-mail hhcc@cybernet.on.ca www.cybernet.on.ca/~hhcc

LAND MANAGER: Haliburton Forest, 705-754-2198, fax 705-754-1179, e-mail halforest@halhinet.on.ca

Rocky Crest Resort

 SOUTH OF PARRY SOUND

Ratings

LENGTH: 12 km (7.5 miles)

TRAIL: Singletrack

SURFACE: Rock outcrops, soft earth, hardpack

TECHNICAL: Moderate to hard

LAYOUT: 3 connected loops, mapped and well marked

TOPOGRAPHY: Canadian Shield rock, mixed forest

AESTHETICS: Elongated slabs of granite, a lookout, and cedar groves, gigantic boulders

IMPRESSION: A romantic retreat with trails

Located at the northwest end of Lake Joseph in Muskoka , Rocky Crest Resort is a deluxe vacation property. Families and couples spend $100 to $160 per person, per night, to stay here, depending on their choice of suite, the day of the week and the season. For their money, they get a luxury condominium unit, a meal plan and a wide range of activities — including mountain biking on 12 km (7.5 miles) of singletrack.

No, you don't have to be a guest to use the trails. But non-guests must pay a day-use fee of $20, which can go toward food and beverage purchases. Between the Cabana Bar, lunch and evening barbecues and the formal dining room, you can easily eat and drink your money's worth — and then some — besides enjoy a rollicking good ride.

Foremost, trails feature Canadian Shield rock. These outcrops jut from the earth like tortoise shells with roundish tops and steep rims. They appear suddenly, intermittently, breaking the leafy canopy, mooning the forest. At times you'll have to pop the front wheel to get on them and lean back low to roll off. Otherwise, they sport minor obtrusions: little ridges, cracks, ripples and depressions. The gray slabs, streaked with bands of white quartz, are elongated with finger extensions. Cairns keep you on course.

Between outcrops is constant change. You'll roam dense woods past decomposing stumps topped with bright mushrooms, through airy hardwoods, fanned with ferns and long tufts of grass. Cedar groves, gigantic boulders, birds galore, and a wind you'll hear but not feel will enlighten the journey.

The resort has three connected loops, each about 4 km (2.5 miles) in length. One leads to a lookout over Lake Joseph, another circumnavigates a lake, and the third, Cathedral Forest, leads through thick, old towering trees. Corduroy logs clear the way over mud, pine needles blanket hardpacked ground while soft areas are riveted with roots.

Status

POLITICS: Rocky Crest Resort is privately owned; trails are also used for hiking and cross-country skiing.

MAINTENANCE: Thank the publishers of *Canadian Cyclist Magazine* for mountain-bike specific trail upgrades and revamps.

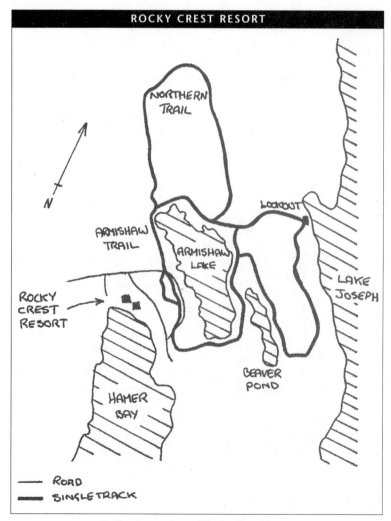

Trail map courtesy of Rocky Crest Resort

Guide Notes

NEAREST COMMUNITY: Parry Sound, Gordon Bay

LOCATION: Located 30 km (19 miles) south of Parry Sound, 2 km (1.2 miles) east off Highway 69 on Hamer Bay Road.

TRAIL MAP: Available on-site.

FACILITIES: Luxury lodging, restaurants, heated outdoor pool, tennis, badminton and basketball courts, fitness center, children's programs, mountain bike rentals, more. Guests have free use of mountain bikes and all visitors can also enjoy canoeing, kayaking, windsurfing, paddleboats — and for an extra fee — sea-dooing and water-skiing.

ADMISSION: $20 for non-guests. Three-night to week-long family packages available.

TIPS: Don't forget your bathing suit.

REPAIR SHOP: Spokeskis, intersection of Highways 11 and 518, has rentals, 705-636-0622. Trysport, 3 Miller Street, Parry Sound, 705-746-8179.

TOURISM INFORMATION: Parry Sound Chamber of Commerce, 800-461-4261 or 705-746-4213, fax 705-746-6537.

LAND MANAGER: Rocky Crest Resort, 800-263-5763 or 705-375-2240, fax 705-375-2210 www.rockycrest.com

Grandview Inn Nature Trails

Grandview Inn Nature Trails

■ □ ◆   HUNTSVILLE, EAST END

Ratings

LENGTH: 15 km (9 miles)

TRAIL: Doubletrack and singletrack

SURFACE: Hardpack with puddles, roots and rock slabs

TECHNICAL: Moderate to hard

LAYOUT: Poorly mapped network of three loops plus spurs

TOPOGRAPHY: Easy rolling hardwood forest, Canadian Shield rock, marshes

AESTHETICS: Red and white spring trilliums, fall colors

IMPRESSION: A scoot through Canadian Shield landscape

Non-guests are welcome to ride the Nature Trails at Grandview Inn. Totaling a 15-km (9 mile) network, they are a mixed bag of doubletrack and single-track, of loops and spurs.

The 5-km (3 mile) Maple Ridge loop is a good place to start. The double-track roams mixed hardwood forest past huge boulders, marshes and a native site where maple syrup demonstrations are staged in spring. The route is hardpacked and rooty, interspersed with slabs of Canadian Shield rock and with successions of puddles, some deceivingly deep. Linked to it is the 2-km (1.2 mile) Deer Run, a singletrack that winds through hilly fields and over granite outcrops.

Tough, technical singletrack is also available — if you know where to look. Rosie's Extension, for example, is a 5-km (3 mile) washboard of roots, rock gardens, and creek crossings. Named after the rancher who broke it in on horseback tours, this unmarked, unmapped offshoot is located just north and east of the native site on the Maple Ridge loop.

Status

POLITICS: Hikers and equestrians frequent trails.

CAUTIONS: Don't rely on the resort's trail map: it's far from scale, out of proportion, and frankly doesn't correspond to what's out there. Also, trails are barely marked and crossed with old logging roads. Be mindful of your turns in case you need to backtrack.

Grandview Inn Nature Trails

Guide Notes

NEAREST COMMUNITY: Huntsville

LOCATION: From Highway 11 North, turn east on Highway 60 in Huntsville and go 5 km (3 miles). The network is on the north side of Highway 60 across from Grandview Inn. Ride up the steep gravel road — just west of the truck weigh station — to the Fairy Vista Trail, a 4-km (2.5 mile) paved path. Hang a left. A head-high sign staked into the ground on your right marks a singletrack that leads the linked loops of Maple Ridge and Deer Run.

TRAIL MAP/INFORMATION: Maps available from the resort's Check-in Desk (note Cautions). Information from Nature Trails at Grandview Inn, 705-789-4417 ext. 3478.

FACILITIES: Mountain bikes available free to guests. The site offers luxury lodging, restaurants, fitness center, golf course, nature programs, and an array of land and water-based sports and activities.

ADMISSION: Free

REPAIR SHOP: Muskoka Bicycle Pro Shop, 14 Main Street E., Huntsville, 705-789-8344.

TOURISM INFORMATION: Muskoka Tourism, 800-267-9700 or 705-689-0660, fax 705-689-9118, e-mail Information@muskoka-tourism.on.ca www.muskoka-tourism.on.ca

LAND MANAGER: Grandview Inn, 800-461-4454 or 705-789-4417. e-mail grandv@vianet.on.ca www.grandviewinn.com

GROUP TOURS: For guests — and non-guests, space permitting — Grandview Inn Nature Trails offers a 1.5-hour riding clinic and tour, Wednesday to Saturday for $15, full suspension bikes provided.

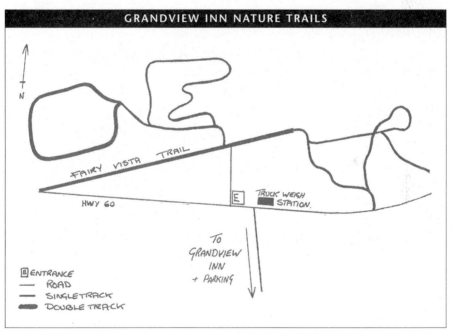

Trail map courtesy of Grandview Inn

Algonquin's Minnesing Mountain Bike Trail

			ALGONQUIN PROVINCIAL PARK

Ratings

LENGTH: 24 km (15 miles)

TRAIL: Wide singletrack

SURFACE: Hardpack with roots, and loose and embedded rocks

TECHNICAL: Moderate to hard

LAYOUT: Four stacked loops of 5, 10, 17 and 24 km (3, 6, 10.5 and 15 miles), mapped and well-marked

TOPOGRAPHY: Expansive hardwood forest, extensive hills

AESTHETICS: Maple leaf canopy, remote lakes, high possibility of moose sightings

IMPRESSION: Rugged wilderness invitation

The Minnesing is a wilderness trail, remote and entirely forested, in the south-central part of Algonquin, Canada's oldest and largest provincial park. It consists of four stacked loops, offering distances of 5, 10, 17 and 24 km (3, 6, 10.5 and 15 miles), each with long hills, mud holes and sections riddled with roots and rocks.

A cross-country ski trail that opened to mountain biking in 1992, the Minnesing is mapped, well marked, one-way and patrolled by volunteer bike rangers. What begins with sand patches soon becomes hardpacked, wide singletrack. As ATVs are used for trail maintenance, the way is as wide as a bobsled run with room to swerve.

The route romps predominantly through sugar maple. The forest is tall, bright and airy with a rich undergrowth of waist-high saplings. The only openings in the high leafy canopy are at two lakes: Polly on the 17-km loop, a pretty place for a picnic, and Linda on the 24-km loop, where you can take a swim and scope for moose. At the top of the 10-km loop is a shelter cabin with picnic tables.

No matter what your distance, prepare for hefty climbs. The farthest loop presents some particularly grueling ascents, while being the prettiest and most technical of sections. Delivering you to one of the highest points in Southern Ontario, it includes four significant uphills — one of them frankly hideous.

Needless the say, descents can howl with speed. The Minnesing's last leg — the final 2 km (1.2 miles) — is especially furious. But loose rocks litter the runway half way down, presenting a floor of marbles that have caused numerous wipeouts.

Overall, the east side is more rugged and rutted than the west. The smoother return traces the old Minnesing Road that once brought rich travelers to the upscale Minnesing Lodge, abandoned in the 1950s.

The trail attracts at least 100 riders on weekends, and about 30 on weekdays, but with everyone flowing in one direction, you'll still find a sense of solitude.

Status

POLITICS: Bike rangers, organized by the Ontario Cycling Association (OCA), patrol the system, assisting riders with minor repairs, helping with trail maintenance and notifying management of heavy windfall. Volunteers are on-site daily during summer, then on weekends to mid-October.

RESTRICTIONS: Biking on the canoe portage routes that cross the trail is prohibited. Riding is not allowed before mid-June.

Algonquin's Minnesing Mountain Bike Trail

Algonquin's Minnesing Mountain Bike Trail

ETIQUETTE: Bikers share a half-kilometer (0.3 miles) trail segment with canoe-carriers on the bottom of the third loop; make yourself known — with their head stuck under a canoe, they can't hear or see your approach. Heed the rules posted at the trailhead. Care to volunteer for the bike patrol? For your time and effort you'll receive free camping; contact OCA, 416-426-7242 www.ontariocycling.org

CAUTIONS: The trail is remote; come prepared with appropriate tools and parts, extra food and lots of water, and know how to deal with mechanical breakdowns. After a rainfall and in early season — until about mid-July — trails are extremely muddy and slippery. Call ahead for conditions.

Guide Notes

NEAREST COMMUNITY: Whitney, Oxtongue Lake, Huntsville

LOCATION: Take Highway 400 north to Barrie, Highway 11 north to Huntsville, then Highway 60 east. The trailhead is located on Highway 60, 23 km from the park's west gate on the left-hand side of the road.

TRAIL MAP: Available at the Visitor's Centre.

FACILITIES: Outhouses and a warming hut at trailhead. Camping at several locations, rental cabins and lodge accommodations, world-renowned canoeing, first-class art gallery, a logging museum, separate hiking trails, Visitor's Centre with outstanding exhibits.

ADMISSION: $10 per vehicle, camping from $15.75 to $22.75. Open mid-June to mid-October.

TIPS: Fall colors traditionally peak on the last weekend of September. Chances of seeing a moose are best in late June or early July. If camping, reserve a spot at Canisbay Campground (705-633-5572), which has ride-in trail access and offers showers. For families, Algonquin also offers a 10-km (6 mile) rail trail from Mew Lake Campground to Rock Lake Campground through fields, forests and alongside three lakes.

REPAIR SHOP: Algonquin Outfitters on Oxtongue Lake on Highway 60 just before the park's west gate (and at two other locations, in Huntsville and at Opeongo Lake in the park), has rentals, 705-635-2243.

TOURISM INFORMATION: Muskoka Tourism, 800-267-9700 or 705-689-0660, fax 705-689-9118, e-mail Information@muskoka-tourism.on.ca www.muskoka-tourism.on.ca

LAND MANAGER: Algonquin Provincial Park, (705) 633-5572.

TOURS: Guided daytrips with Algonquin Outfitters, 705-635-2243, www.algonquinoutfitters.com

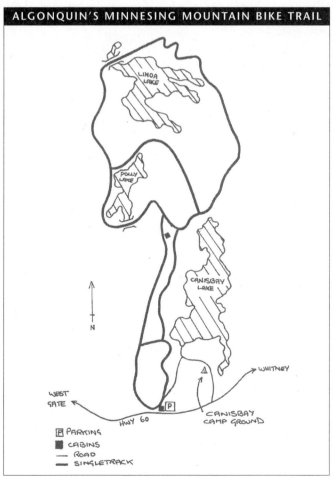

Trail map courtesy of Algonquin Provincial Park

New York

Spencer Park

Holiday Valley, Holimont, and Rock City

⓪ (40)

 ◆◆◆ ELLICOTTVILLE

Ratings

LENGTH: 22 miles (35 km)

TRAIL: Singletrack, doubletrack ski access roads, old logging roads, cleared slopes

SURFACE: Hardpack singletrack with roots, rocks; rocky doubletrack

TECHNICAL: Hard to extreme

LAYOUT: Trails on two adjacent ski hills and a 7-mile (11 km) stretch of the Finger Lakes Trail with offshoots and logging road options

TOPOGRAPHY: 740-foot (225 meter) ski hills and hilly, rugged state forest

AESTHETICS: High views, optional hike in Little Rock City, great dining and party town

IMPRESSION: The place to bike in Western New York

Holiday Valley Ski Resort offers a 4-mile (6.5 km) loop, up and down its slopes and across its forested backside. It also links to trails at Holimont, a private ski resort, and to a 7-mile (11-km) stretch of the Finger Lakes Trail (FLT) through Rock City State Forest. This is the only place besides Letchworth State Park in all of New York State where bikers are allowed on the amazing long-distance hiking trail.

Riding the "Valley" begins with a long, hard climb on a doubletrack ski access road to the top of Cindy's Chair. Singletrack then welcomes you with a twisty, rooty, rocky romp through woods, west to the top of the Tannenbaum Chair. From here, you can careen down the slope to complete a loop, or carry on to the communications tower to set wheels on the white-blazed, singletrack, FLT.

At the trail intersection, a right turn will take you to Holimont. Look for the property line trail, which forks to the left off the FLT. It forms an 8-mile (13 km) singletrack loop with some great downhills through woods and meadows. Holimont also offers a 4-mile (6.5 km) network of doubletrack cross-country ski loops. However, you need permission to ride Holimont; respect the resort's "ask first" proviso.

Alternatively, a left turn at the communications tower, takes you across a dirt road onto a severely technical section of the FLT. Unless you're sporting superb balance and a good sense of humor, follow the road instead, left (east), then right (south) on McCarthy Hill Road. After 1.5 miles (2.5 km) on McCarthy, veer left onto an old, overgrown logging road, blocked by large boulders, and follow it through a small clearing to a fun singletrack descent.

After half a mile (1 km), you'll rejoin the FLT at the foot of a rocky descent. Turn left onto another logging road, follow for another half-mile (1 km), then exit right, down a long, water-bar filled descent to Hungry Hollow Road and the site of an old Civilian Conservation Corps camp. Cross the road, following the white blazes on an ever-steepening climb to a rocky traverse that eventually leads to Little Rock City, an area of house-sized boulders.

The FLT runs around the rocks while a yellow-blazed, hiking-only side trail weaves through them. From here, the FLT continues west to Stone Chimney Road while a new blue-blazed trail — built by the Western New York Mountain Biking Association (WNYMBA) — runs a long descent east back to Hungry Hollow Road.

Status

POLITICS: The FLT in Rock City State Forest is always in danger of being closed to bikes. To keep it open, WNYMBA has put in hundreds of maintenance hours repairing the worst-drained, muddiest section — from the communications tower north to Holimont. In addition, in an effort to distribute use away from the heavily used FLT, WNYMBA and the New York State Department of Environmental Conservation (NYSDEC) are laying out many new trails throughout this area; contact WNYMBA or Mud, Sweat and Gears bike shop for new trail updates.

RESTRICTIONS: Stay off the golf course at Holiday Valley. Don't bike Holimont without asking first, then pick up a free permission slip from the general manager, 716-699-4907. Little Rock City is off-limits to bikes.

ETIQUETTE: Avoid the FLT when wet and don't skid the steep sections.

EVENTS: Holiday Valley is site to a Wednesday night race series, a mid-summer Roots, Rocks and Ridges race, and a Fall Festival Mountain Bike Race.

MAINTENANCE: Continued access to the FLT is contingent on bikers maintaining the trail in good condition. Also, help is needed for the cutting of new trails.

CAUTIONS: Midway through the FLT, a succession of water bars on a big downhill section have been site to some nasty, helmet-crunching, endos. Ride this downhill slowly until you learn to judge the dynamics of these bumps.

Guide Notes

NEAREST COMMUNITY: Ellicottville, Salamanca

LOCATION: From I-90 West out of Buffalo, take Route 219 past Ellicottville to Holiday Valley Ski Resort. The resort loop starts at the Training Centre; from Route 219 turn west on Holiday Valley Road (at the Inn at Holiday Valley) and take your first left up to the building. Park in the lot and ride uphill on the ski access road to your left. To reach Holimont from Ellicottville, go west 1 mile (1.6 km) on Route 242 and follow signs.

TRAIL MAP: A detailed map can be downloaded from WNYMBA, www.buffnet.net/~jsundqui/hol1.gif

FACILITIES: Ellicottville offers excellent dining and a slew of aprés biking bars. There's a wide variety of lodging in town. Holiday Valley itself has an inn and a rental pool of condos, 716-699-2345 www.holidayvalley.com

ADMISSION: Free

TIPS: Stop at Mud, Sweat and Gears bike shop for ride suggestions.

REPAIR SHOP: Mud Sweat and Gears, 28 Munroe Street, Ellicottville, 716-699-8300. Limited rentals at the Inn at Holiday Valley.

TOURISM INFORMATION: Ellicottville Chamber of Commerce, 716-699-5046. Cattaraugus County Tourism, 800-331-0543.

LAND MANAGER: Holiday Valley, 716-699-2345. Holimont, 716-699-4907. Rock City State Forest, New York State Department of Environmental Conservation, 716-665-6111.

GROUP RIDES: WYNMBA (see Appendix B).

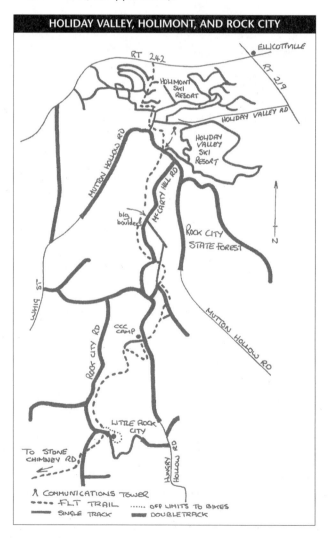

Alleghany State Park (41)

 SALAMANCA, EAST OF JAMESTOWN

Ratings

LENGTH: 21 miles (34 km)

TRAIL: Wide corridors with a singletrack in their middle

SURFACE: Hardpacked track in a grassy lane

TECHNICAL: Easy to moderate

LAYOUT: Network of five cross-country ski loops

TOPOGRAPHY: Hilly, forested mountain

AESTHETICS: Vista, healthy hardwood forest, and wildflowers

IMPRESSION: A weekend destination for an aerobic roller coaster, plus a variety of outdoor pursuits

At Alleghany State Park, mountain bikers are granted use of 21 miles (34 km) of cross-country ski trails that form five interconnected loops on the top and southern slope of a completely leaf-canopied mountain.

All trails are wide grassy corridors with a singletrack down their middle. Tracks are clean and smooth with few rocks and no roots. Wet and muddy sections, however, are found throughout. Turns everywhere are big and gradual. Some hills are steep.

The top offers winding rollers and a vista, while the slope, with its nearly 900-foot (270 meter) drop in elevation has grand, fast descents and sustained, arduous climbs. The hardwood forest is mature with thick trunks and high tops. The setting is bright, open and airy with wildflowers, birds and scampering critters everywhere.

The park is big and beautiful with forested mountains, lakes, caves and a bizarre geological rock site. As a destination for a variety of outdoor pursuits, it offers a paved bicycle path and separate trails for hiking, backpacking, and horseback riding.

Status

POLITICS: Mountain biking is only allowed on the shared-use trails in the Art Roscoe Ski Touring Area, but the Western New York Mountain Biking Association (WNYMBA) is actively working on opening other trails to bikes.

ETIQUETTE: With big hills and wide corridors, it's easy to forget that trails are shared-use and not bike-only; rules of the trail apply.

EVENTS: Raccoon Rally, annually at the end of June, attracts over 750 riders, organized by WNYMBA, events include cross-country and downhill races, fun rides and kid's races, 716-655-3364, e-mail racrally@wnymba.org

MAINTENANCE: WNYMBA puts in a lot of man-hours on trail maintenance at this park.

CAUTIONS: Make sure your brakes are in good working order.

Guide Notes

NEAREST COMMUNITY: Salamanca, Ellicottville, and Jamestown

LOCATION: From Highway 219 south of Buffalo, continue south to Salamanca, then west on Route 17 and follow park signs. The summit trailhead for the Art Roscoe Ski Touring Area is 1.5 miles (2 km) past the entrance on ASP. Route 1, though you can also park at the base of the mountain off ASP Route 2.

TRAIL MAP: Available at the park entrance.

FACILITIES: Camping, cabin and cottage rentals, washrooms, showers, beaches, snack bar, restaurant, camp store, interpretive programs, museum.

ADMISSION: $4 per car day fee. Tent sites $13, cabins $31 to $67, and limited full-service cottages rent for $100.

TIPS: For good dining and aprés biking festivities, visit Ellicottville.

REPAIR SHOP: Mud, Sweat and Gears, 28 Monroe Street, Ellicottville, 716-699-8300. Limited rentals available on-site.

TOURISM INFORMATION: Cattaraugus County Tourism, 800-331-0543.

LAND MANAGER: Alleghany State Park, 716-354-9121, reservations: 800-456-CAMP, www.park-net.com

GROUP RIDES: WNYMBA (see Appendix B).

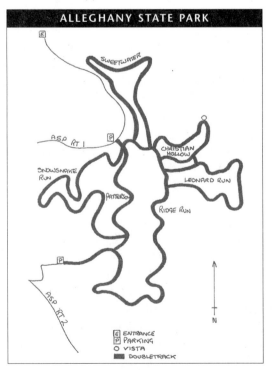

Sprague Brook Park (42)

Ratings

LENGTH: 6 miles (10 km)

TRAIL: Groomed wide singletrack

SURFACE: Hardpack and muddy sections

TECHNICAL: Easy to moderate

LAYOUT: Four separate trails

TOPOGRAPHY: Rolling hardwood forest

AESTHETICS: Deer, birds, brook

IMPRESSION: Fun and dry though not extensive

Sprague Brook is a little county park with four short but sporty trails.

In the east, a cross-country ski loop offers a fern-framed, fast track that rolls through hardwood forest under a leafy canopy. Wide and smooth, the eastern trail unravels with knolls and turns. While merely 2 miles (3 km) in length, it's an invigorating circuit, worth a few laps.

In the west, from the bridge over Sprague Brook, a rollicking singletrack on the brook's bank follows the downstream flow to the park's boundary. On the other side of the bridge, a rugged snowmobile track climbs through woods and alongside fields. At its top, a spur leads to a cliff edge overlooking the brook. Birds galore flit through the forest and deer can often be seen.

In the northern hinterlands, behind the campground area, singletrack links with a pipeline trail that is always laced with mud holes.

Status

POLITICS: Sprague Brook is one of only two legal riding areas in Erie County. Hikers frequent trails.

Guide Notes

NEAREST COMMUNITY: Glenwood, East Concord

LOCATION: From Route 240 (which runs just east and parallel to Highway 219), turn east on Footes Road (between Glenwood and East Concord) and go 0.6 miles (1 km). Entrance is on your left-hand side.

TRAIL MAP: www.buffnet.net/~jsundqui/sb.htm

FACILITIES: Camping, washrooms, sports fields, tennis courts, picnic tables.

ADMISSION: Free

REPAIR SHOP: Backcountry Bikes, 21 Elm Street, East Aurora, 716-655-3545.

TOURISM INFORMATION: Buffalo Visitors Centre, 800-283-3256.

LAND MANAGER: Sprague Brook Park, 716-592-2804, www.erie.gov/parks

GROUP RIDES: WNYMBA (see Appendix B).

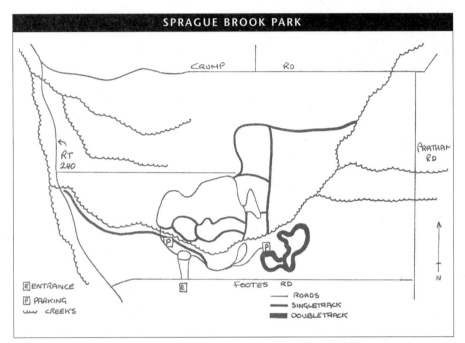

Trail map courtesy of the Western New York Mountain Biking Association

Erie County Forest

SPRINGVILLE, SOUTHEAST OF BUFFALO

Ratings

LENGTH: 6 miles (10 km)

TRAIL: Singletrack, snowmobile trails, and dirt roads

SURFACE: Hardpack, soft rutted soil, mud

TECHNICAL: Moderate

LAYOUT: Network of loops and spurs

TOPOGRAPHY: Hilly forest, pine plantation, creek crossings

AESTHETICS: Deep, dark woods

IMPRESSION: Aggressive messy maze

When you bike Erie County Forest, you bite back. It calls for aggressive exploration. There's too much shade for sunglasses, too much mud for cruising and too many dead ends for continuity.

The broken network consists of singletrack trails, cross-country ski loops, snowmobile track, firebreak corridors and dirt roads. Most paths are wide, straight and rutted. Many areas are mucky. The forest, a mix of pine plantation and sugarbush, is thick with trunks and mosquitoes.

Encompassing property on either side of Genesee Road, Erie's south wing is four times as big as its north. You'll find rugged, rooty, singletrack loops with out-and-back spurs in the north.

In the south, a ski loop ambles among pines. A dirt road — a scenic lane for beginners — climbs to a plateau where several straight firebreak trails radiate through dark woods to property lines. Onwards, the road descends to a creek crossing where a snowmobile trail veers off to a succession of beaver dams. Halfway to the dams a link connects to other out-and-back, hilly options.

The nicest, driest, most inviting trails of all are unfortunately off limits to bikes. These are the yellow-blazed nature trails and orange-blazed Finger Lakes Trail. They used to be open, but access was lost due to overuse by bikes during the rainy summer of 1992.

Status

POLITICS: This is one of two legal riding sites in Erie County.

RESTRICTIONS: Yellow- and orange-blazed trails are off-limits to bikers.

ETIQUETTE: The clay-base soil retains water; avoid for at least two days after a rainfall.

CAUTIONS: Trails are used illegally by ATVs.

Erie County Forest

Guide Notes

NEAREST COMMUNITY: Sardinia, East Concord

LOCATION: From Highway 219, go east on Genesee Road. The parking lot is about 5 miles (3 km) past East Concord (at Highway 240) on the left-hand side of the road. Trails lie on both sides of the road.

TRAIL MAPS: www.buffnet.net/~jsundqui/ecf.gif

FACILITIES: Washrooms, parking lot. Camping nearby at Sprague Brook Park (see page 135), 716-592-2804.

ADMISSION: Free

REPAIR SHOP: Backcountry Bikes, 21 Elm Street, East Aurora, 716-655-3545.

TOURISM INFORMATION: Buffalo Visitors Centre, 800-283-3256.

LAND MANAGER: Erie County Department of Parks and Recreation, 716-496-7410, www.erie.gov/parks

GROUP RIDES: WNYMBA (see Appendix B).

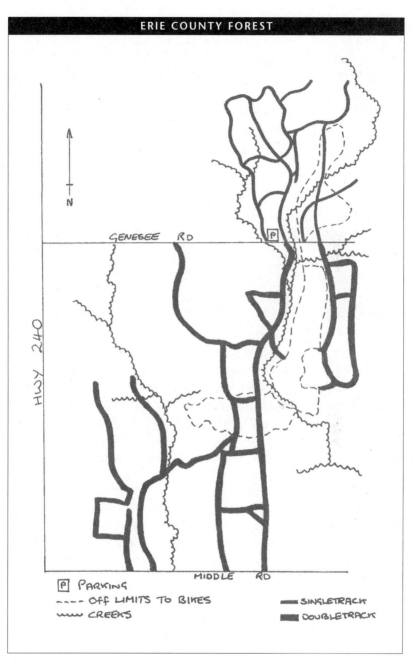

Trail map courtesy of the Western New York Mountain Biking Association

Letchworth State Park

(44)

 MT. MORRIS, SOUTH OF ROCHESTER

Ratings

LENGTH: 42 miles (68 km)

TRAIL: Singletrack and doubletrack

SURFACE: Varies

TECHNICAL: Easy to extreme

LAYOUT: Trails on either side of a 600-foot (180 meter) gorge, including a 22-mile (35 km) stretch of the Finger Lakes Trail

TOPOGRAPHY: Relatively flat, lush forest laced with streams and ravines

AESTHETICS: Astounding views of the Genesee Gorge, three major waterfalls, trail variety, other activities

IMPRESSION: An awesome destination for all levels

Letchworth is a 17-mile-long (27 km) state park that encompasses both sides of a 600-foot-deep (180 meter) gorge carved by the snaking Genesee River. Stop at a lookout to see sheer walls, waterfalls, and the brown bottom flow that continues to wear the floor deeper. The park offers more than a dozen marked and mapped multi-use trails — from a flat railbed to a technical gully — for a total of 20 miles (32 km) of track on both sides of the gorge. The Visitor's Centre will provide you with a map, indicate which trails are open to riding — not all are — and give suggestions. (Note well: Trail 1, along the west edge of the gorge — a crowded tourist track — is not open to bikes.)

The pick of the park, however, is its additional 22-mile (35 km) section of the Finger Lakes Trail (FLT), on the east side of the Genesee. Letchworth is the one of only two spots in all of New York where mountain bikers can legally ride on the incredible FLT, a long-distance hiking trail that streaks across the state and has five extensive branch lines.

Opened to bikers on a trial basis in 1996 — and still regarded as a pilot program — FLT riding is extremely tough and technical. You can't ride without stopping and likely can't ride without falling. Certain spots are impossible to pedal, and continual dares will have you pushing your limits.

The trail is narrow, winding and rugged with — yes, roots and rocks, but — namely, countless ravine crossings. The ravines, cut by streams that feed the Genesee, are 5- to 35-feet deep (1.5–10.5 meters). And steep, with V-and U-shaped gouges and tricky, rock-filled water bottoms.

As you ride parallel to the gorge, ravines cut the trail at about five-minute intervals. Crossing is a tricky in-and-out, down-and-up affair that's often straight without mercy. Even some switchbacks are brutal.

Letchworth State Park

The most technical section is in the center, between the 16- and 22-mile markers; mileage counters are posted on trees and the trail is marked with yellow blazes. While completely forested, the FLT also offers numerous side trails to the rim of the gulf for a view. The north end has lots of poison ivy, the south end is less used.

Status

POLITICS: The FLT is patrolled by the National Mountain Bike Patrol of Western New York. The bike patrol was instituted as a condition for the opening of the trail.

RESTRICTIONS: Riding is permitted only from June 1 to October 1, and not after heavy rains. Permits are required to ride the FLT, available free on a self-service basis at major trailheads; good for a year, but must be carried at all times.

ETIQUETTE: Do not cut across switchbacks on ravine crossings. Don't skid or ride when wet. Do not ride the FLT outside of park boundaries. Ride only where permitted; not all trails are open to bikes.

EVENTS: The park offers interpretive bike hikes on select trails throughout the season. Begun in 1997, this program attracts 25 riders on average.

MAINTENANCE: The FLT section in Letchworth is maintained and supported by the Rochester Bicycling Club and the Western New York Mountain Bike Association.

Guide Notes

NEAREST COMMUNITY: Mt. Morris, Warsaw, Geneseo, Castile, Portageville.

LOCATION: From I-90 south of Rochester, go south on I-390 to Exit 7 (at Mt. Morris), continue south on Route 408, turn right on Route 36 to the park's north entrance. (If coming from Buffalo take Route 400 south to Route 20A east to Route 36 south to the park entrance.) To access the FLT, take Route 36 south from the entrance to Chapel Road, turn right, continue 2.5 miles (3.8 km) to Mt. Morris Dam Road, turn right. The Mt. Morris Trailhead, where permits can be acquired, is on your right hand side. To access other parking lots along the length of the FLT, continue on and take a right fork on River Road.

TRAIL MAP: Available at the Visitor's Centre, and on internet, www.buffnet.net/~jsundqui/letch1.gif

FACILITIES: Camping, cabin rentals, hot air ballooning, whitewater rafting, horseback riding, swimming pools, museum, Glen Iris Inn and Restaurant, picnic shelters, hiking-only trails, interpretive programs, reservations.

ADMISSION: $4 per car day-fee, camping $15, rental cabins vary with ranging prices up to $83 for units with heat, water and electricity. Open for riding only from June 1 to October 1.

REPAIR SHOP: Swain Ski & Sports 131 Main Street, Geneseo, NY, 716-243-0832 or 800-836-8460; has rentals.

TOURISM INFORMATION: Wyoming County Tourism, 716-493-3190, fax 716-493-3191, e-mail wctpa@wycol.com. Greater Rochester Visitors Association, 800-677-7282 or 716-546-3070, fax 716-232-4822, e-mail grva@frontiernet.net

LAND MANAGER: Letchworth State Park, 716-493-3600 (Park Office), 800-456-2267 (reservations).

GROUP RIDES: RBC and WNYMBA (see Appendix B).

Rattlesnake Hill �45

DANSVILLE, SOUTH OF ROCHESTER

Ratings

LENGTH: 10 miles (16 km)

TRAIL: Doubletrack

SURFACE: Gravelly, hardpacked fire roads

TECHNICAL: Easy

LAYOUT: Disjointed network

TOPOGRAPHY: Forested hills, fields, ponds

AESTHETICS: Ponds, birdhouses and birds galore including great blue herons

IMPRESSION: An aerobic workout or family nature ride

Rattlesnake Hill is a wildlife management area with fire roads streaking through it. The property is mostly covered with mature woodlands and conifer plantations, but there are also overgrown fields, old-growth apple orchards and a handful of diked ponds.

The fire roads are hardpacked, well-drained, sprinkled with gravel and closed to vehicles. Wide, with some big ups and downs, they offer vigorous training rides, and also non-technical family touring on sun-bathed corridors.

There are a few out-and-back routes along with one big loop, though numerous other loops can be formed with connections on quiet country roads. Moreover, dikes along ponds are rideable, and though short, offer sightings of great blue heron, ducks, geese, and other birds among the reeds and lily pads.

Ignore freshly bulldozed passageways that branch from roads; they just present muddy, ugly trouble. The park's only singletrack trail is overgrown and not worth an ounce of effort. Stick to the roads, do a couple of hard laps, and keep your eyes peeled for wildlife, including white-tailed deer, cottontail rabbits, wild turkey and ruffed grouse.

Status

CAUTIONS: The park is open to hunting in spring for turkey and in fall for deer; wear bright colors.

Rattlesnake Hill

Guide Notes

NEAREST COMMUNITY: Dansville

LOCATION: From I-390 south of Rochester, take Exit 5 at Dansville and take Route 36 south to Route 436 west. Go 7 miles (11 km) to Shute Road, turn left, go 1 mile (0.6 km) to Walsworth Road, turn left, follow to end where you'll find a parking lot. From here, bike 0.6 miles (1 km) west on Ebert Road to the second yellow gate to enter.

TRAIL MAP: Available from Land Manager.

FACILITIES: Parking

ADMISSION: Free

REPAIR SHOP: Swain Ski & Sports, 131 Main Street, Geneseo, 716-243-0832 or 800-836-8460; has rentals.

TOURISM INFORMATION: Greater Rochester Visitors Association, 716-546-3070 or 800-677-7282, e-mail grva@frontiernet.net

LAND MANAGER: NYSDEC (New York State Department of Environmental Conservation), 716-226-2466.

GROUP RIDES: Rochester Bicycling Club (see Appendix B).

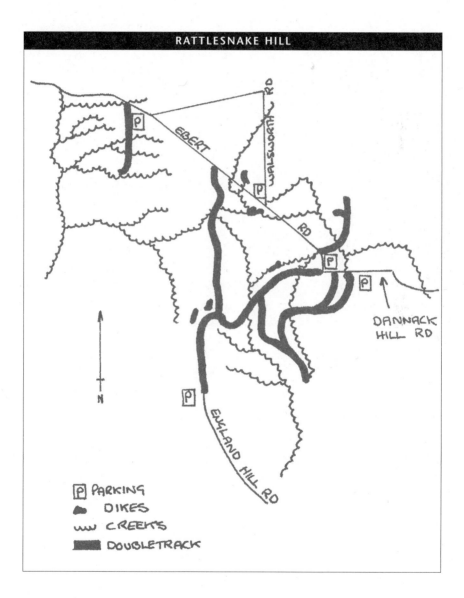

Spencer Park

 HONEOYE, SOUTH OF ROCHESTER

Ratings

LENGTH: 12 miles (20 km)

TRAIL: Singletrack and doubletrack

SURFACE: Well-drained hardpack with roots, moguls

TECHNICAL: Moderate to extreme

LAYOUT: Unmarked, unmapped array of singletrack trails and doubletrack cross-country ski network

TOPOGRAPHY: Mixed forest, rolling terrain, steep pitches

AESTHETICS: High lake view, whoop-de-doos

IMPRESSION: Spirited with a real high fun factor

Ride hard or go home. Singletrack trails at Spencer Park — officially Harriet Hollister Spencer State Recreation Area — are not made for dawdling. The spunky spurs off the cross-country-ski doubletrack were designed by hard-core riders.

Trails twist through tight tangles of trees and run slalom courses around trunks. They lean on banks, charge over stutter-bumps and swoop among bike-eating moguls. Ravines, steep climbs, scary descents, jump points and off-camber segments all add to the antics.

Moreover, trails are enhanced by apparatus. There's a giant S-shaped ramp with banked turns, a hollowed-out tree, and a couple of chest-high rock piles. Log obstacles are not just singular logs, but peaked stacks. And yet, throughout, the only real snags are nasty, unexpected, endo-inducing stumps and roots — which have been marked with fluorescent orange paint.

There are seven singletrack trails. None take longer than 20 minutes and all lead back to the doubletrack or the park's main access road. The doubletrack itself offers a good, hardy ride on hilly, bumpy gravel. Forming 6 miles (10 km) of connected loops, and used as a racecourse, the winding doubletrack can translate into a 30-mph (50 kph) runway for those who crank it.

Status

ETIQUETTE: Don't ride when it's wet. Whatever you carry in, carry out.

EVENTS: The Spencer Park Challenge, annual summer race, organized by Towners, 716-271-4553.

MAINTENANCE: Trails are maintained by Towners' (bike shop) race team, and the New York State Section V Ski League.

CAUTIONS: Be vigilant for fluorescent orange blotches and steer clear of them. Trails are two-way; mind your corners. The park is open to deer hunting in fall; dates are posted at the entrance.

Spencer Park

Spencer Park

Guide Notes

NEAREST COMMUNITY: Honeoye, Avon, Canandaigua, and Naples

LOCATION: From I-390, take Exit 10 at East Avon and go east 4.5 miles (7 km) on Route 5/20. Turn south on Route 15A and go 8.5 miles (13.5 km) to 20A. Turn left and go east 4 miles (6.5 km) to County Road 37. Turn right and go south 9 miles (14.5 km) to entrance on your left. Trails are accessible from the first parking lot or from the one at the end of the entrance road.

TRAIL MAP: A cross-country ski map of doubletrack trails only, is available from the Land Manager.

FACILITIES: Parking

ADMISSION: Free

REPAIR SHOP: Swain Ski & Sports, 131 Main Street, Geneseo, 716-243-0832 or 800-836-8460, has rentals. Towners, 1040 University Avenue, Rochester, 716-271-4553.

TOURISM INFORMATION: Greater Rochester Visitors Association, 716-546-3070 or 800-677-7282, e-mail grva@frontiernet.net

LAND MANAGER: Finger Lakes State Park Region, 607-387-7041, fax 607-387-3390.

GROUP RIDES: Rochester Bicycling Club (see Appendix B).

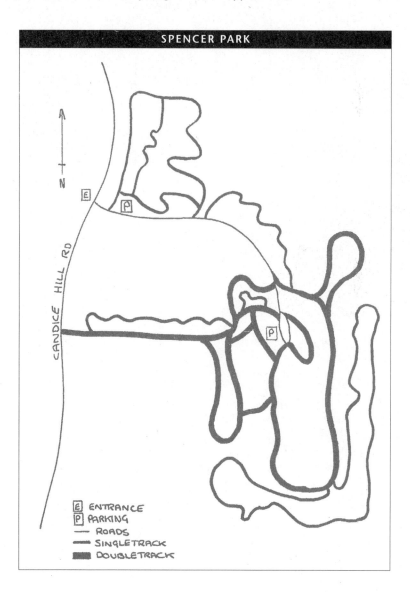

New York
CENTRAL

Bear Swamp

Bear Swamp

47

■ ◆ NEW HOPE, SOUTHWEST OF SYRACUSE

Ratings

LENGTH: 13 miles (21 km)

TRAIL: Wide and narrow singletrack and doubletrack

SURFACE: Hardpack with roots, rocks and rocky fire roads

TECHNICAL: Moderate to hard

LAYOUT: Mapped, marked network of cross-country ski loops and fire roads and unmarked singletrack

TOPOGRAPHY: Very hilly, mixed forest with a creek and wetland

AESTHETICS: Lookouts over wetland and Skaneateles Lake

IMPRESSION: Extensive sweat ground with bomber downhills

Bear Swamp has major hills: fast long descents and killer payback climbs. Its network of mapped cross-country ski loops present hardpacked, wide single-track with roots and rocks. Trails scale and funnel through steep forested slopes, but also streak along ridgelines.

Three doubletrack fire roads, with loose and embedded rocks, offer riding that's less technical, though not less hilly. They also provide quick links between loops and shortcuts to the parking lot.

Trails on the map are marked — sometimes with boulders and slate rock pillars at junctions — but not all trails are marked on the map. Recently forged singletrack trails, yours to discover, also snake narrowly through the property.

Completely forested with pine, spruce, larch and hardwood, Bear Swamp is rectangular shaped with a creek running through its middle. The creek spills into a large marsh in the south, and not to be missed is a trail to a look-out over the marsh with its birdhouses, balsam fir, swamp-meadow grass and alder patches. Another highlight is the ridge run in the east, which provides views between trees of Skaneateles Lake and its valley far below.

Status

POLITICS: This state forest is logged, and work crews with tractors and bulldozers may be encountered. Moreover, portions of trails may be chewed into ugly, unwieldy corridors. Hikers and equestrians frequent trails.

ETIQUETTE: Avoid the only singletrack that stems from the parking lot — the lot behind Colonial Lodge — unless conditions are dry. The track, which runs parallel to — and within earshot of Route 41A — is poorly drained and muddy. Sign your name at the registration billboard.

Guide Notes

NEAREST COMMUNITY: New Hope, Skaneateles, and Cortland

LOCATION: From Skaneateles, southwest of Syracuse, take Route 41A south to New Hope and continue 4 miles (6 km) to where the road veers right while a dirt road leads straight. Follow the dirt road (behind the Colonial Lodge) to the parking lot on your left.

TRAIL MAP: Cross-country ski trail maps are available in a box at the trailhead under the registration billboard.

FACILITIES: Three separate parking lots.

ADMISSION: Free

TIPS: Prefer to end with a downhill rather than heart-pounding climb? Park at the lower lot: continue south past Colonial Lodge on Route 41A to Iowa Road, turn left, follow to end, turn left and continue to the lot.

REPAIR SHOP: Bike Loft, 717 South Bay Road, North Syracuse, 315-458-5260.

TOURISM INFORMATION: Greater Syracuse Chamber of Commerce, 800-234-4797 or 315-470-1904, www.syracusecvb.org

LAND MANAGER: NYSDEC (New York State Department of Environmental Conservation), 607-753-3095.

GROUP RIDES: CNY Dirt (see Appendix B).

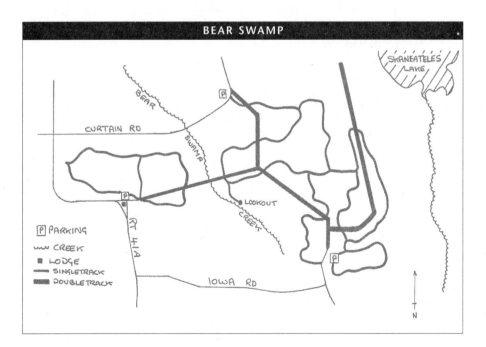

Highland Forest

48

■■■◆■■ SOUTHEAST OF SYRACUSE

Ratings

LENGTH: 23 miles (37 km)

TRAIL: Mix of singletrack and doubletrack

SURFACE: Hardpack with rooty sections, muddy spots, beds of loose slate and smooth whoop-de-doos

TECHNICAL: Moderate to hard

LAYOUT: Mapped, marked network of cross-country ski loops and a mountain bike specific-designed trail

TOPOGRAPHY: Forested hills and valleys

AESTHETICS: Stately trees, vistas, ridges, ravines

IMPRESSION: Extensive and popular with big ups and downs and technical outbursts

Within its 15-mile (24 km) perimeter, Highland Forest encompasses a wooded jumble of high hills and low valleys. All trails involve climbing and offer screaming descents. Winding singletrack do-si-dos with straight doubletrack. Lowlands are muddy and intermittent red pine groves have litters of roots.

Biking is allowed on the 23-mile (37 km) network of shared-use, cross-country ski loops. These are mapped and marked — though not as well as they could be.

Beginning from a small clearing behind the park office, trails radiate in four directions. Further afield, they intersect and branch while a maze of maintenance roads offers links between routes.

Trails run ridgelines, bomb down hills, streak through muddy valleys and present both gradual and steep killer climbs. The best trail is the East Rim. Designed by mountain bikers for mountain bikers, it features a near-mile (1 km) twisty, swoopy downhill with large, smooth kinetic humps.

Status

POLITICS: Highland Forest is the most bike-friendly park in Central New York — thanks to the efforts of CNY Dirt (see Maintenance). Mountain biking is on shared-use trails that are frequented by equestrians; hikers also use portions.

RESTRICTIONS: Separate hiking trails, marked by black dots on the map, are off limits to bikes.

ETIQUETTE: Avoid the West Trail, which is particularly popular with equestrians.

EVENTS: Bikeloft Highland Forest Classic, an annual since 1991, attracts 350 competitors, features an 8-mile (13 km) course.

Highland Forest

MAINTENANCE: CNY Dirt puts a lot of volunteer labor into trail maintenance — removing logs, pruning trees and building waterbars. The club is working on rerouting lowland trails to less muddy ground.

Guide Notes

NEAREST COMMUNITY: Fabius, Cazenovia

LOCATION: From I-81 south of Syracuse, take Exit 14 and go east 10 miles (6 km), turn right on the Main Park Road, go 2 miles (3 km) to the main parking lot across from the Park Office.

TRAIL MAP: Available in the park office and at the self-serve registration box.

FACILITIES: Parking, separate hiking trails

ADMISSION: $1. Open from May to mid-November.

REPAIR SHOP: Bike Loft, 717 South Bay Road, North Syracuse, 315-458-5260.

TOURISM INFORMATION: Syracuse Convention and Visitors Bureau, 800-234-4797 or 315-470-1910 www.syracusecvb.org

LAND MANAGER: Highland Forest, 315-683-5550.

GROUP RIDES: CNY Dirt (see Appendix B).

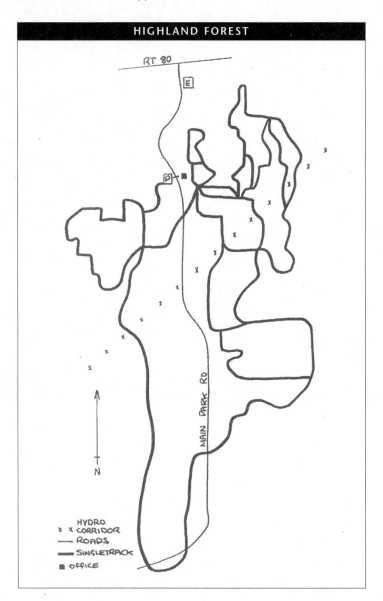

Stoney Pond

■ ◆ SOUTH OF ONEIDA

Ratings

LENGTH: 13 miles (21 km)

TRAIL: Singletrack

SURFACE: Hardpack with rooty sections

TECHNICAL: Moderate

LAYOUT: Network of loops

TOPOGRAPHY: Forested slopes around a pond

AESTHETICS: A pond, wooden bridges, old stone property lines

IMPRESSION: A peaceful invitation

Stoney Pond State Forest is a sloped property with a pond in the bowl of its ladle. Multi-use trails form interconnected loops on the forested slope and around the pond. They are hardpacked singletrack trails with switchbacks, swooping undulations and steep pitches. Every sweet long downhill comes with a stiff payback climb. The track is twisty with rooty sections and minor muddy spots, but much is savoringly smooth.

The access road, with two parking lots, cuts across the middle of the slope, offering initial uphill track to the west and downhill to the east. Go down. See Stoney Pond, a pretty teardrop body of water dotted with little islands bursting with wildflowers. It's the park's focal point, drawing visitors to fish, picnic, canoe, hike, birdwatch and camp. Even so, the place is calm, quiet and not heavily used.

The loop around the pond runs along a sun-drenched dike, then through woods with a smattering of wooden bridges over streams. From the pond's circumference, five trails branch up and away to surrounding high ground. Old stone property lines, including an enduring slate wall, lay former claims throughout the park. The forest includes plantations of red, white and Scotch pine, Norway spruce, and hardwoods of sugar and red maple, black cherry, white ash and beech.

Stoney Pond

Status

CAUTIONS: Trails are two-way; mind blind corners. Logging takes place in the forest; you may encounter fresh cut stumps, broken roots and piles of branches. Don't swim in the pond — it contains a high duck fecal count.

Guide Notes

NEAREST COMMUNITY: Cazenovia, Morrisville

LOCATION: From I-81 south of Syracuse, take Exit 15 and take Route 20 east to Nelson. In Nelson, turn right on Erieville Road (also County Route 67) across from the Nelson Inn, and go 1.3 miles (2 km). Turn left on Old State Road and go 2.5 miles (4 km). Turn right on Jones Road and go 1.3 miles (2.1 km) to the shoulder parking lot on your left. Trails lie on both sides of the road.

TRAIL MAP: Available from the Land Manager.

FACILITIES: Parking lot, outhouses, 14 camp sites — including a site on an island; for permits, 607-674-4036.

ADMISSION: Free

TIPS: Wear insect repellent.

REPAIR SHOP: Bike Loft, 717 South Bay Rd, North Syracuse, 315-458-5260.

TOURISM INFORMATION: Syracuse Convention and Visitors Bureau, 800-234-4797 or 315-470-1910 www.syracusecvb.org

LAND MANAGER: NYSDEC (New York State Department of Environmental Conservation) Division of Lands and Forests, 607-674-4036.

GROUP RIDES: CNY Dirt (see Appendix B)

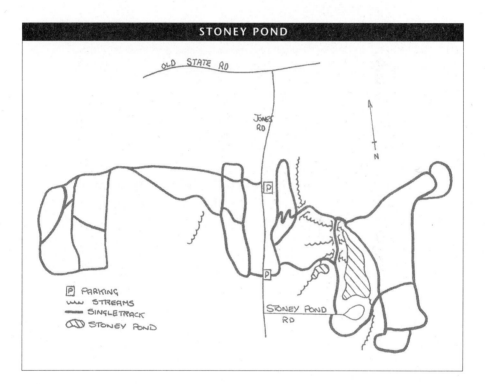

Vanderkamp Center (50)

Ratings

LENGTH: 15 miles (24 km)

TRAIL: Singletrack

SURFACE: Hardpack with roots, rocks, mud holes and old roads

TECHNICAL: Hard to extreme and easy dirt roads

LAYOUT: Marked, mapped, color-coded network

TOPOGRAPHY: Forested with small hills, creeks, a lake and beaver pond

AESTHETICS: Narrow boardwalk, relics, changing forest

IMPRESSION: Tight and twisty as can be

Vanderkamp is a technical creation of fat-tire love. Much of the 15-mile (24 km) network of strict singletrack is the product of three years toil by CNY Dirt members Dave Sheldon, his wife and two friends.

In 1995, with approval to re-establish old neglected trails on privately owned land of a Protestant church camp, the avid mountain bikers cleared, mapped and blazed a splendidly entertaining playground. The Munchkin-Muffin loop, for example, has land mines of rocks, steep little cranks, acute turns, and off-camber log piles.

To keep trails tight and squirrely with technical bites, few trees were cut. Roots, ruts, logs, mud holes, handlebar-width squeaks through trees and creek crossings on bridges, planks and corduroy logs keep you busy, challenged and amused.

You'll pass an old sulfur spring with a stone ruin, lean-tos, cabins, old trail signs, and a tree growing through the rusted rim of a carriage wheel. An old boardwalk, three planks wide, winds the length of a football field over a marsh. It's fanned with overgrowth, has lots of angles, including a few tricky turns, along with several broken and sagging boards. The plantation, in the property's middle, features a straight-line succession of smooth whoop-de-doos through a stage of majestic pines.

Three dirt roads cut across the rectangular 1,100-acre (440 ha) property. Trails form loops, links and a plethora of intersections between them. All are marked with color-coded plastic tabs, and moreover with numbers at intersections that correspond to numbers on the map. The middle section is easier than the ends. But in this dense network you'll never be more than a 30-minute walk from your car — should you have a mechanical breakdown. The earth is soft in spots; it's not as hardpacked as it will be, once Vanderkamp — a relatively unknown biking domain — gets "discovered."

Status

POLITICS: Open year-round, Vanderkamp Center is a Christian retreat that is host to youth groups, conferences, weddings, team training programs and more. Trails are used by hikers, and horseback riders are being considered. If equestrians are granted access, the network may be selectively partitioned.

ETIQUETTE: Register your name on a clipboard inside the main doors of the office on your left, and drop a donation in the box for land use and trail upkeep.

Vanderkamp Center

Guide Notes

NEAREST COMMUNITY: Cleveland

LOCATION: From I-81 north of Syracuse, take Exit 32 and go 13 miles (21 km) east on Route 49. Turn left (north) on Martin Road and go 1.6 miles (2.6 km) to the entrance on your left.

TRAIL MAP: Detailed maps available at the office.

FACILITIES: Parking, washrooms, lake for swimming, boat rentals, campsites, RV facilities, cabins, B&B-style lodges.

ADMISSION: By donation. Campsites $10, cabins and lodges for groups, minimum 6 to 15, $25–$90.

REPAIR SHOP: Bike Loft, 717 South Bay Road, North Syracuse, 315-458-5260.

TOURISM INFORMATION: Syracuse Convention and Visitors Bureau, 800-234-4797 or 315-470-1910.

LAND MANAGER: Vanderkamp Centre, 315-675-3651, fax 315-675-8802, e-mail vk2@juno.com

GROUP RIDES: CNY Dirt (see Appendix B).

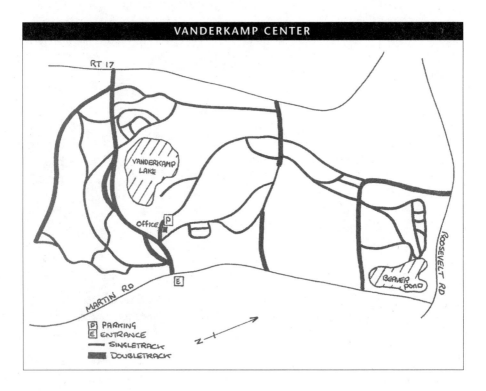

Barnes Corners

■ ◆ SOUTHEAST OF WATERTOWN

Ratings

LENGTH: 15.5 miles (25 km)

TRAIL: Singletrack and doubletrack

SURFACE: Hardpack with roots, rocks and grassy corridors with mud holes

TECHNICAL: Moderate to hard

LAYOUT: Marked, mapped, looped network

TOPOGRAPHY: Hilly mixed forest, marshy lowlands, gulf rim

AESTHETICS: Views of a gulf with a waterfall, birds and mushrooms galore, blackberries, raspberries, and ferns

IMPRESSION: Sensational variety

Rodman-Barnes Corners Ski Trails features an intoxicating 3-mile (5 km) rollercoaster of smooth whoop-de-doos. Head east to west for a slight grade in your favor and little pedaling is required to swoop like a skilled skier through the extended succession of hippo-high humps. Woo-hoo!

This exalting rodeo — on the Inman Gulf Glide and John Young Trails — is enhanced with a view. On your immediate right lies Inman Gulf, a 300-foot-deep (90 meter) ravine. At the first of many lookouts, you can see far, far below, the snaking Gulf Stream that carved the cavity, and the formidable cliffs it left in its wake. Further along is a view of Rainbow Falls, a long, loud plunge of water on the face of the sheer rock wall.

Elsewhere in Barnes Corners, trails weave through mixed hardwoods and stately pines. They run alongside creeks and marshes, over bridges, under hydro lines and across grassy, bushy fields. Most are hardpacked singletrack with varying degrees of roots, rocks, dips and log obstacles.

The fields, however, are overgrown, wet and rutted corridors with hordes of flies and raspberry bushes. While corduroy logs offer some ease-of-travel, deep mud holes remain.

Hills are sporadic, often steep and sometimes rocky. Prepare to pay a price in mud, sweat and scratches to reap the park's sweeter treats. Trails are well marked with arrows, names and even information signs about flora and fauna.

Barnes Corners

Status

POLITICS: One of many state forests on the Tug Hill Plateau allowing mountain biking.

RESTRICTIONS: The Oak Rim Trail, which extends west from the John Young Trail, is off-limits to bikes.

Guide Notes

NEAREST COMMUNITY: Tremaines Corners, Barnes Corners

LOCATION: From I-81, south of Watertown take Exit 42 and go east on Route 177. The trailhead and parking lot is on the left-hand side of the road, 2 miles (3.5 km) past the hamlet of Tremaines Corners.

TRAIL MAP: Can be obtained from the NYSDEC (see Land Manager).

FACILITIES: Parking lot

ADMISSION: Free

TIPS: To bypass a nasty field crossing and launch straight into the whoop-de-doos, park on Williams Road, at its easternmost shoulder lot. South of the park, on the other side of Route 177, a 2.5-mile singletrack beelines to a smaller selection of Jefferson County Ski Trails.

REPAIR SHOP: The Bike Shop, 1035 Arsenal Street, Watertown, 315-788-1820.

TOURISM INFORMATION: 1000 Islands International Tourism Council, 800-847-5263 or 315-482-2520, e-mail info@1000islands.org www.visit1000islands.com

LAND MANAGER: New York State Department of Environmental Conservation, 315-376-3521.

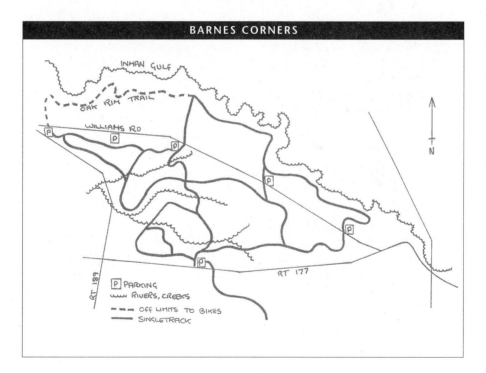

Appendix A

Ontario Cycling Association

Formed in 1973, the Ontario Cycling Association (OCA) is the officially recognized provincial sport organization for cycling in Ontario. The OCA has a mandate to promote cycling in the province through Participation, Advocacy, Competition and Education (PACE). The OCA is a member organization with an office located in central Toronto.

The Ontario Recreational Mountain Bicycle Alliance (ORMBA) is a committee within the OCA structure that deals with MTB advocacy issues across the province. Its mission statement is "Access through Education." ORMBA is the voice of MTB advocacy in Ontario and offers, through its volunteer network, assistance on dealing with trail closures, a trail maintenance manual, and trail maintenance clinics around the province. On the education side, ORMBA trains and certifies MTB Instructors, operates Learn to MTB clinics, and has an adopt-a-trail program that encourages groups to form volunteer assistance bike patrols.

ORMBA also has a formal Volunteer Ranger Training Program which has been used by IMBA (the International Mountain Bicycling Association) to train patrolers for their National Mountain Bike Patrol. The program is used by Algonquin, Lower Trent and Dundas Valley Volunteers.

The OCA and ORMBA are affiliated with IMBA. Membership with OCA includes membership in ORMBA and also a 30 percent discount on Via Rail, 10 percent discount on parts and accessories at various cycle shops, and a free subscription to Pedal Magazine, among perks.

OCA's annual handbook, *Cycling in Ontario*, which is sent to members and is available free at most cycle shops, is an invaluable resource to events, tours, races, clubs, trail updates, hot spots and more.

OCA membership is $35 for individuals or $40 for families. For more information, contact OCA, 416-426-7242, fax 416-426-7349, e-mail ocycling@istar.ca www.ontariocycling.org

Or mail your request for information, including your name and mailing address, to:

Ontario Cycling Association
1185 Eglinton Avenue E., Suite 408,
Toronto, Ontario
M3C 3C6

Appendix B

New York Mountain Biking Coalition

The New York Mountain Biking Coalition (NYMBC) is the voice of the New York mountain biker at the state level. It is an association of local and regional clubs around the state fighting for trail access. NYMBC's mission is to provide leadership on state-wide issues, while letting local groups act on gaining and preserving access to local trails. NYMBC representatives deal directly with other NY user groups, including hikers and equestrians.

NYMBC is on the web at www.ggw.org/NYMCB/ and can be reached at 716-655-5130 or e-mail ny-mtb@cycling.org

To get involved with NYMBC, get involved with your local MTB group. NYMBC has only club members, not individual members. The clubs active in trail access issues in the areas of NY covered by this book are the Western New York Mountain Biking Association (WNYMBA), the Rochester Bicycling Club (RBC), and CNY Dirt.

These groups have been active in opening or keeping open the NY rides described in this book. They have worked with land managers, hiking groups, and the woods themselves to do what it takes to get and keep trails open to bikes. "Doing what it takes" includes a great deal of volunteer trail maintenance work, getting the word out on threatened closures, and negotiating rules and policies in order to allow bikes. In many cases, they have been able to gain permission to put in many miles of new trails, trails designed by bikers for bikers. They also do a lot of riding, and are the ones to contact when you want to find new places to ride.

WYNMBA is the group fighting for trail access throughout Western New York since 1992. Beyond advocacy, WNYMBA leads regular group rides, and puts on the largest mountain bike race and festival in New York, the annual Raccoon Rally in Allegany State Park. Tel 716-655-3364, e-mail wnymba@cycling.org   www.wnymba.org

RBC, with 650 family memberships, runs regularly scheduled road and off-road rides March through October. Maintenance days, skills clinics and weekend tours are also organized. Tel 716-723-2953, e-mail info@rbcbbs.win.net   www.win.net/~rbcbbs

CNY Dirt, a Central New York mountain bike club and advocacy group with 100 members, organizes regular group rides, April to mid-November, along with maintenance days, skills clinics and weekend trips. Tel 315-458-5260, e-mail bikeloft@juno.com   www.thebook.com/dirt